THE TRI
GOD'S
KINGDOM IN THE
MILLENNIUM
AND END TIMES

A PROPER BELIEF FROM THE TRUTH IN SCRIPTURE AND CHURCH TEACHINGS

BY JOSEPH IANNUZZI, OSJ

St. John the Evangelist Press
222 S. Manoa Rd.
Havertown, PA 19083 USA
Phone: 610-853-9801 Fax: 610-853-9802

IMPRIMI POTEST:
Rev. Vito Calabrese. O.S.J., Superior General,
Oblates of St. Joseph Congregation, Rome, Italy(March 8, 1999)

ISBN: 0-9670102-0-9

Published by:
    St. John the Evangelist Press
    222 South Manoa Rd.
    Havertown, PA 19083 USA

Cover Design by A.J. Kenny

Printed in the United States of America
"In God We Trust"

How to Order Additional Copies of this Book:

To place an order for this book, please contact the bookstore
or catalog from which it was originally purchased. If not,
call toll-free:

St. Andrew's Productions
1-888-654-6279
www.saintandrew.com
or write to:
St. Andrew's Productions
6111 Steubenville Pike
McKees Rocks, PA 15136

Quantity discounts are available to individuals for
evangelization purposes. Please call for rates.

Important Note to Christian Readers

Please judge the contents of this book only after you have read it completely. If you have a preconceived notion about Christian denominations other than your own, you will make a serious mistake if you use this prejudice as an excuse not to read the important scriptural and historical information contained in this book.

> For the scripture says, "No one who believes in him will be put to shame." For there is no distinction between Jew and Greek; the same Lord is Lord of all, enriching all who call upon him. For "everyone who calls on the name of the Lord will be saved" (Rom. 10:11-13).

All direct and indirect scriptural citations are from the *New American Bible,* St. Joseph's Edition, Catholic Book Publishing Co., NY, 1987, unless otherwise noted.

Dedication

This book is dedicated and consecrated to the Holy Spirit and to his beloved spouse the Blessed Virgin Mary. May it be a source of enlightenment and encouragement to all truth seeking Christians who aspire to holiness in God's Kingdom.

Author's Acknowledgments

I'd like to express my sincere gratitude towards the editor A.J. Kenny, my father, my superiors, my professors at the Gregorian University in Rome and in the United States, and all those who pray for priests, that God's Will may be accomplished through them.

Publisher's Acknowledgments

We would like to thank Bridget Hylak and the staff of Come Alive Communications, Inc. (www.comealiveusa.com) for their excellent editing and word processing skills. (Come Alive, the "Multilingual Catholic Experts", P.O. Box 436, West Grove, PA 19390 USA, Tel: (610) 869-3660.)

PREFACE

Recently, much talk concerning the imminent return of Christ — the "Parousia" or the "Day of Judgment" — has led to spiritual apathy in those who hold that such "gloom-and-doom" nonsense leads to pessimism. Some who are not as interested in these current topics tend to gauge the validity of matters by relying on the strict definitions of the Holy See, instead of engaging in subjective discussions on people and events about which the Church has prudently refrained from making any definitive pronouncement.

Both these attitudes, while acceptable, have left in their wake a real confusion. We cannot overlook what needs to be tested and discerned (even before the Church has expressed her official recognition), and fail to compare this to the corpus of Tradition; because this can lead to a dangerous reduction in the progression of transcendent truth.

Since Catholic Tradition holds that all ecclesiastical approbations or recognitions come by way of ongoing prophetic contributions from the Church's hierarchy and laity alike, there is little room for any skepticism toward prophetic revelation when it is genuine: "Christ... fulfills this prophetic office not only by the hierarchy... but also by the laity. He... provides them with the sense of faith [*sensus fidei*] and the grace of the word" (*Catechism of the Catholic Church*, Libreria Editrice Vaticana, St. Paul Books & Media, 1994, 904). Thus, a policy of strict repression of all matters hitherto not officially recognized by the Church, not only contrasts with her traditional position, but stifles the growth of prophetic doctrinal development.

Indeed, during the times of the Old Testament prophets and even at the time of Christ, the believing faithful were consistently receptive to the Spirit's divine action. Acting upon it out of a sense of obedience, they assisted the Church's hierarchy in a fuller discovery of the truth. Over the centuries, the believing faithful, in virtue of their fidelity of witness, have manifestly exercised their prophetic office with discretion in obedience to God and to his Church; by this means, they have enriched the Church in her formulated dogmas and magisterial teachings.

It is this long-standing Tradition, this *sensus fidei,* that I have chosen to incorporate into this book. My purpose is not simply to treat for the first time the doctrines on the "millennium" as contained in Sacred Scripture, Tradition and the Magisterium; more significantly, this work will speak to the believing faithful through whom the Spirit operates as the Church continues in her discovery of "the fullness of truth" (Jn. 16:13).

Since all truths necessarily abide within the confines of obedience to the wisdom of the Church's hierarchy, this book likewise adheres to the same pattern of respect to proper authority. Moreover, since all truths that have proceeded from the Spirit have always been ordered so as to harmoniously aid in the edification and embellishment of Christ's mystical body, what better way to do so than by way of this long-standing Tradition? This I have sought to do through the presentation of those doctrines surrounding the controversial term commonly called "millenarianism." At the request of the editor, I have addressed, for the first time, this popular concept with no references to private revelation — even though several exist, fully approved by the Church, which second her Tradition. The three sources, therefore, contained in this book are quite simple and simultaneously profound: Sacred Scripture, Tradition and

Magisterial teachings.

May this book prove advantageous to those truth-seeking Christians who look forward to the coming of God's kingdom!

PUBLISHER'S RESEARCH NOTE

This work breaks from the standard research style and tradition, and includes the full citation immediately after the appropriate sentence or paragraph where it is necessary to give proper credit or authority. This allows the reader to immediately see the importance, relevance and timeliness of the citation without stumbling to the back of the book or to the bottom of the page. We hope this "user-friendly" break from style will encourage other publishers to follow suit.

After the first citation to a reference source, the standard *Ibid.* is used to refer to the citation thereafter. A Bibliography is also included at the back of the book.

If you cannot find a citation listed, please contact the Publisher.

Please note that all italics or bold lettering found within citations of others are done for emphasis by the author, the Rev. Joseph Iannuzzi.

TABLE OF CONTENTS

CHAPTER 1

INTRODUCTION

In his recent Apostolic Letter *Tertio Millennio Adveniente,* (*Tertio Millennio Adveniente,* in Inside the Vatican, Martin de Porres Printshop, New Hope, KY, 1994) Pope John Paul II stated that Christianity is on the threshold of a "new springtime" of life. This springtime, a unique renewal in Christendom, is all the more striking in view of its close link to the year 2000. And this is best summed up in the following quotations of the Supreme Pontiff: "The Magisterium... has certainly made a significant contribution to the preparation of that *new springtime of Christian life* which will be revealed by the Great Jubilee..." (*Tertio Millennio Adveniente, Ibid.,* 18); "The Second Vatican Council is often considered as the beginning of a new era in the life of the Church" (*Ibid.*); "He (Blessed Hannibal DiFrancia) saw in the 'Rogate' [prayer of supplication] the means God Himself had provided to bring about that 'new and divine' holiness with which the Holy Spirit wishes to enrich Christians at the dawn of the third millennium, in order to 'make Christ the heart of the world'" (Letter on the Centenary of the Rogationist Fathers, Pope John Paul II, in *L'Osservatore Romano,* Vatican City, English Ed., July 9, 1997, p. 3).

The Pontiff's vision of a fruitful season in Christianity was shared by one of his predecessor's, Pope John XXIII, who foresaw that the Church would "increase the reign of the Divine Savior" through a sovereign act of almighty God. Choosing the Latin word *amplificet* which signifies not only an "increase" but also the "accomplishment" or "fulfillment" of Christ's reign, Pope John XXIII's vision appeared as the basis of John Paul II's recent statement. What John Paul II considered "the Magisterium," John XXIII called "the Church". Nonetheless, in both instances, the arrival of a new, increased and fulfilled reign of Christ in the world is consistently prophesied. In fact, in this same Apostolic Letter, Pope John Paul II outlines what will be one of the most fervent of all the Church's petitions: "during this important time, as the eve of the new millennium approaches... unity among all Christians of the various confessions will increase until they reach full communion" (*Tertio Millennio Adveniente, Ibid.*, 16).

While the Holy Father stresses the essential quality of the Savior's redemptive Passion, Death and Resurrection, he nonetheless impresses upon all Christians their paramount duty: that of assisting the pilgrim Church in her historical progression through a "new evangelization" which will culminate in "the glorification of the Trinity" (*Ibid.*, 55). By dedicating the three final years of this millennium to the three Divine Persons of the Trinity, the Jubilee celebration makes present "the goal and *fulfillment* of the life of each Christian and the whole Church in the Triune God" (*Ibid.*). According to Cardinal Joseph Ratzinger, this fulfillment finds its roots in the eighth chapter of the Letter to the Romans where St. Paul speaks very plainly of all creation groaning in anxious expectation of the sons of God. The Cardinal states: "And we hear today the groaning as no one has *ever* heard it before... The Pope does indeed cherish a great expectation that the millennium of divisions will be followed by *a millennium* of unifications. He has in some sense the vision that... now, precisely at the end, we could rediscover a new unity through a great common reflection" (*On the Threshold of a New Era,* Cardinal Joseph Ratzinger, Ignatius Press, San Francisco, CA, 1996, p. 231).

The *Catechism of the Catholic Church* (*CCC*) further points out that in her Sacraments and institutions, the Catholic Church groans and travails among creatures in anxious expectation of the revelation of the sons of God (*CCC, Ibid.,* 671). This groaning "as no one has ever heard it before" increases as the Church approaches ever nearer to that great and universal day in which God's incomprehensible love for his bride will be made manifest to the "sons of God".

Following the same Spirit, the Church Fathers set the precedent by conferring certain characteristics upon this "millennium of unifications" of which the Holy Father speaks. Such characteristics unanimously imply the unity of creation; the outpouring of God's munificent fruits; lasting peace and security; harmony; abiding justice; and the transformation of the nature of time (no more regulation of days and nights — no more darkness but only light).

Whatever the characteristics may be, in order for such a great and universal millennium to occur, there must first exist the workings of the Divine Agent who alone is capable of heralding in this *new springtime*. This Agent, the Catholic Catechism tells us, is none other than the Holy Spirit through whom Christ operates. It is the continuous and sanctifying work in the Church, wrought by the actions of the Redeemer and through the operations of *the Holy Spirit* that enables us, sons of God, to cry out *"Abba, 'Father'...* so that we may be glorified in him" (Rom. 8:15-16).

It is noteworthy that this sanctifying work of the Redeemer, whose operations are possible only through the Holy Spirit, the *Sanctifier,* cannot effectively herald in the *new springtime* except by internalizing the external laws. According to Apostolic Tradition, the Old Testament laws given to Moses and handed down throughout the centuries will come alive within the hearts of all Christians. Far from being external, this event will imbue all creation with an interior impulse of love, consequently effecting the living, dynamic characteristic of the "law of love," or "law of freedom" (*Summa Theologica*, St. Thomas Aquinas, editio quarta, Lethielleux, Parisiis 1939, Ia-IIae, qu.107, art. 1, ad 2; Jm. 1:25; 2:12). It will no longer be we who live, but Christ who lives in us. He will free us from the "principle at war with the law of our minds, taking us captive to the law of sin that dwells in our members" (cf. Rom. 7:23). Once the unity of creation is perfectly realized, all creation will no longer groan but enjoy the freedom of the sons of God who live by a law inscribed upon their hearts.

As the Catechism tells us, the Agent responsible for this internalization is the Spirit of God at work in us in a "new," dynamic and impulsive way. For just as the Spirit filled the entire Upper Room at Pentecost in an impetuous driving wind, and enkindled love within the hearts and minds of the Apostles by parting into tongues of fire, so this same Spirit will renew the face of the entire earth purifying it with fire and enkindling love within the hearts of its inhabitants (cf. Acts 2:2-3).

For centuries the Catholic Church has consistently taught of this renewal of all creation, for which all things groan in anxious expectation. Evidenced throughout Scripture, in the writings of the Apostolic Fathers and Magisterial documents, the undisputed *deposit of faith* will be the central focus and basic argumentation of our critique on the millennium, also known as the *temporal or millenary kingdom*. Availing ourselves of these three sources necessary for the formulation of doctrine, we will attempt to unravel the tangled web of millenaristic doctrines and determine where they conform with Church teachings.

To ensure a methodic and comprehensive treatise on this subject, the specific doctrines of the Apostolic Fathers that refer to the *renewal* or to the *millennium* will be completely explained. After all, the Apostolic Fathers enjoy the reliability and authority of a non-speculative discipline, commonly known as *Positive theology*.

Holy Mother Church teaches us that, through the combined lights of reason and divine revelation, this branch of science avails itself of the three aforementioned sources of revelation: *Sacred Scripture, Tradition* and their interpretation by the living *Magisterium* of the Church. Needless to say, *Positive theology* differs considerably from *Speculative theology* inasmuch as the former studies the data of revelation with a critico-historical method, and the latter with the light of reason illumined by faith alone. The positive method, we can therefore say, is a more reliable science insofar as it ascertains knowledge of the facts while avoiding theories based upon pure *speculation.* And it is precisely here that we discover the assurances of our faith.

The writings of the Apostles and their disciples constitute one of the most reliable sources of Catholic Tradition. The Catholic Catechism acknowledges these doctrines, whose positive contributions have enriched the Church throughout the centuries: "Indeed, the Church, though scattered throughout the world, even to the ends of the earth, having *received the faith from the Apostles and their disciples...* guards [this preaching] with care, as dwelling in a single house, and similarly believes as if having but one soul and a single heart, and preaches, teaches, and hands on this faith with a unanimous voice, as if possessing only one mouth" (*CCC, Ibid.*, 173).

When referring to "disciples", the Church is here directing our attention to that apostolic witness contained especially in the writings of the Church's Fathers. In fact, while quoting the Church Father, Saint Irenaeus, the Catholic Catechism also attests to the integral contribution that he and many other Fathers made to her Tradition (cf. *CCC, Ibid.*, 78, 688).

Let us now examine these apostolic doctrines handed down to the Apostolic Fathers — that corpus of followers who have been entrusted with the task of faithfully transmitting the apostolic teachings of Christ to the Church.

CHAPTER 2

THE CHURCH FATHERS SPEAK

APOSTOLIC FATHERS

The Catholic Church defines the *Apostolic Fathers* as those "towering intellects of the early centuries of the Church, whose writings, sermons and holy lives influenced dramatically the definition, defense and propagation of the Faith" (*Catholic Encyclopedia*, Sunday Visitor Pub., Huntington, IN, 1991, p. 399); "those Christian writers who lived near enough to apostolic times to have had personal communication or dealings with the Apostles, or at any rate to have come within their near and *unmodified* influence"(*Catholic Dictionary,* Macmillan Co., 1941, p. 32). From a broader perspective, the *Early Church Fathers* are described as "all those writers of the first twelve centuries whose works on Christian doctrine are considered of weight and worthy of respect... More strictly those of the first twelve, and especially of the first six centuries, who added notable holiness and complete orthodoxy to their learning" (*Catholic Dictionary, Ibid.*, p. 200).

From these definitions, and indeed, from sheer reputation itself, the preeminent role played by the Fathers in the Church's formulation of doctrine is clear. They are the last representatives of an ancient era, whose theological and literary contributions have influenced all ecclesiastical literatures which followed them, and indeed, Tradition itself. Schooled

9

and educated by the best teachers of classicism, they placed the fullness of their talents, at the service of the Catholic Church. Far from resting on their literary laurels, the Apostolic Fathers utilized both written and verbal expertise, and even such God-given gifts ranging from rhetoric to apologetics to simple sermons. The result of their varied efforts undoubtedly furnished the Church with her pure orthodox doctrines on matters of faith and morals.

Among this inspired group of ecclesiastical writers, we find the *Church Doctors*. Indeed, it would be unthinkable not to mention these renowned men and women not only by reason of their holiness, but for their orthodoxy of doctrine and their eminence of knowledge. Though they followed the Apostolic Tradition of the Fathers, the *Church Doctors* are different for three reasons: a) they need not have lived in ancient times; b) their education is required to have been extraordinary so as to merit the praise of the *Doctor Optimus, Ecclesiae sanctae lumen* ("Excellent Doctor, light of the holy Church"); c) it is required that this title be conferred on them in a sufficiently explicit way [a solemn act of the Pope] (*Catholic Dictionary of Dogmatic Theology,* Bruce Publishing Co., Milwaukee, WI, 1952, pp. 80-81).

Having clarified the role of both of these important categories of teachers, let us begin our treatise of the Apostolic Fathers' doctrines concerning the renewal of Christianity. In doing so, we will address such questions as, "Did the Apostolic Fathers ever mention an 'era of peace' or an intermediary reign of Christ on earth?" And, "Are they unanimous on the nature of God's Kingdom on earth? Do their teachings concur with those of Church Doctors or with her Magisterium?"

These and other questions will be dealt with in a clear and concise way, revealing intriguing answers and assisting us in arriving at the fullness of the truth.

Papias, Church Father (floruit ca. 130 A.D.)

In examining the triumphant renewal of Christianity, many authors have assumed a scholastic style, and have cast shadows of doubt on the early writings of the Apostolic Fathers. Many have come close to labeling them as heretics, mistakenly comparing their "unmodified" doctrines on the millennium to those of the heretical sects. Obviously, the Fathers, who received their doctrines from the Apostles themselves, some of whom are referred to either in Scripture or by the Fathers as "presbyters" (referred to in the original Latin as "presbyteri", and translated into English as *elders* or *seniors*), therefore obtained their eminent teachings from Holy Mother Church herself.

In launching their unwarranted attack, most of these authors manifest their lack of experience in the disciplines of Positive and Dogmatic theology. To the detriment of avid truth-seeking Christians, the opinions disseminated throughout these works are tantamount to certain mainstream speculative theologians who propagate ideas which are at times inconsistent with Church teaching.

As an illustration, consider the following excerpt from one such book, which contains one of the most common objections raised regarding the Apostolic Fathers' doctrines. The book states the objection as follows:

> Both Justin and Irenaeus misunderstood the first century Father Papias to have claimed he received a Millennium doctrine personally from the Apostle John. But as the historian Eusebius of Caesarea makes clear in his *Historia Ecclesia,* Papias himself is candid that he did not directly hear of the apostles speak about a millennium, nor their disciples either, but rather of their "acquaintances".

The theory that Papias of Hierapolis, the Catholic Church Father, Bishop and Martyr, drew all his information from "acquaintances" and not directly from the Apostles, has always been just that — a "theory". And so it remains to this day. Based on plausible logic, some have hastily concluded that Papias alludes to having never received any dictation nor direct information from John the Apostle.

This claim, however, is pure conjecture. Those who advance this theory base their conclusion on Eusebius. Whenever faced with an historical dilemma, Eusebius, one of several Church historians, is accorded the rare authority to speculate in order to provide the faithful with a practical and relevant theological response. This by no means guarantees the historical validity of such speculation, but merely puts the issue aside until further doctrinal development assists in its clarification.

It is the speculative claim of this *historian* that Papias received his information from what the supporters of this theory have labeled "acquaintances". However, Papias himself designates them as "presbyteri" (seniors). Therefore, it is indeed possible to question the "infallibility" of their speculative theology in the assessment of Church history. Let us examine the words of Papias himself to better determine whether he credits "acquaintances" as providing him with his information.

So far as you are concerned, I shall not hold back a single thing I carefully learned from *my seniors (presbyteri)* and carefully remember, and *shall thoroughly guarantee the truth of these matters.* For I do not delight in wordy accounts, as many people do, but in accounts that tell *the truth.* Furthermore, I do not take delight in the commandments of anybody else, but in *those* mentioned as having been given by the Lord for our belief and which proceed from Truth itself.

Whenever anyone came my way, who had been a follower of *my seniors,* I would ask for the accounts of *our seniors:* what did Andrew or Peter say? Or Philip or Thomas or James or John or Matthew, or any other of the Lord's disciples?... For, as I see it, it is not so much from books as from the living and permanent voice that I must draw profit (The Fragments of Papias, Papias of Hierapolis, nn. 3-4, in *The Fathers of the Church,* CIMA Publishing Co., NY, 1947, p. 374).

Clearly, those whom Papias calls "my seniors", among whom are several of the Apostles, others have taken the liberty to call "acquaintances". Obviously, a senior is hardly comparable to a mere acquaintance. To further emphasize this point, it must be noted that the Apostolic Father and Saint, Irenaeus of Lyons, employed the same term as that of Papias, "presbyteri", thereby denoting consistent authoritative personages entrusted with guarding the Apostolic Tradition in its entirety and the governance of Christian communities. When referring to the new springtime of Christianity and to the temporal kingdom (springtime, like the temporal kingdom, is a seasonal flourishing that leads to summer's brightness), Irenaeus addresses his readers with the following: "His Kingdom, when the just will rule on rising from the dead; when creation, reborn and freed from bondage, will yield an abundance of food of all kind from the heaven's dew and the fertility of the earth, just *as the seniors recall (quemadmodum presbyteri meminerunt)*" (Adversus Haereses, Irenaeus of Lyons, V.33.3.4., *The Fathers of the Church,* CIMA Publishing Co., NY, 1947, pp. 384-385).

Both Papias and Irenaeus recall those personages whom the Catholic Church has always held in high esteem and recognized as "leaders" of the early Christian community. Although *presbyteri* was a title given to both the Apostles and a small group of wise leaders, Papias is very explicit that he was referring to the former by stating, "What did Andrew or Peter... or Philip or Thomas or James say?"

Scripture scholars point out that in the Acts of the Apostles, where *seniors* are mentioned for the first time, not only is a distinction made between their role [*presbyteros*] and that of the Apostles [*apostolos*] (cf. Acts 15:2.6.23), but their function is explained as one of safeguarding the Apostolic Tradition and governing the Christian community (cf. Acts 20:17-35). In fact, the author of Acts (most likely St. Luke) refers to presbyters as *episkopoi* (Acts 20:28), and St. Peter the Apostle modestly refers to himself as a presbyter (*syspresbyteros:* 1 Pt. 5:1).

While Acts 20:17 and 1 Pt. 5:1 both share the original Greek title of "presbyter", they don't necessarily imply a sharing in the same office. Neither is the office of *episkopos* in Acts, in the technical and ecclesiastical sense of the word, the office we nowadays refer to as the episcopate, the office of Bishop. The presbyters were a group of holy and wise elders of the early Christian community who, although appearing to lack the faculties to absolve others of their sins (Jas. 5:16), safeguarded the Apostolic Tradition and governed the flock entrusted to them. Saint Paul, unlike Saints Peter and Luke, never refers to the elders in his epistles as *presbyteros* but as *diakonos*, thereby emphasizing perhaps the most important function of their office: service toward neighbor, especially within the household of God. The author of the "pastoral letters", on the other hand (it is uncertain whether he is the same Paul of the epistles), describes the office of *presbyteros* whose purpose is to form, guide and organize the Christian community: as leaders, they are to preach and teach (1 Tm. 5:17).

However, it is impossible to deny that *presbyteros* was also a title given to the Apostles themselves; the Fathers bear witness to this. In the face of the apparent confusion on the usage of the title *presbyteros,* recent biblical scholarship aids us in understanding its twofold definition. It is evident that "pastor" was a title that assumed various names, among which were *episkopos, presbyteros* and *diakonos*. The title *episkopos* was given to those who fulfilled an office whose nature was never clearly defined (functions varied between those of administrator, leader of the community, power to consecrate, etc.). The titles *presbyteros* and *diakonos* were given to those entrusted with the care of God's flock.

While it is true that *presbyteros* was a personal title given to the Apostles, it also developed into an honorific title for a "college" that had the explicit obligation of safeguarding the faith and governing God's flock. Whenever we hear of the early Church Fathers referring to *presbyteros,* therefore, it is understood that they are referring to both the Apostles and to the college instituted for the welfare and maintenance of the members and faith of the early Christian community.

Tradition, moreover, clearly manifests that "seniors" were not merely passing "acquaintances", but well-known faithful Christians, holy and wise in the accurate recall of the Apostolic Tradition, who lived in the company of the Apostles and carefully understood their teachings.

Papias deliberately and emphatically insists on the veracity of his writings, as we have seen. Just as the Evangelist Mark interpreted and faithfully penned Peter's recounts without ever having heard nor followed the Lord, likewise Papias is known to have conveyed with doctrinal accuracy the Gospel of St. John. Papias, moreover, never denies having received dictation from John the Apostle, he simply mentions that he was instructed by his *seniors,* and goes on to name some of them who were Apostles. As Holy Mother Church tells us, Papias, who served as Bishop of Hierapolis of Greater Phrygia from 60 A.D to 125 A.D., faithfully conveyed John's Gospel under the Apostle's dictation: "Papias by name, of Hierapolis, a disciple dear to John... copied the Gospel faithfully *under John's dictation"* (*Codex Vaticanus Alexandrinus,* Nr. 14 Bibl. Lat.

Opp. I., Romae, 1747, p. 344). What, then, do we make of the opinions of those who contend that Papias never received dictation from John, as their theory directly contrasts with this Vatican-issued statement?

Indeed, one would then find oneself at a loss, particularly after stumbling across other ecclesiastical statements in the same vein: "The last of these Evangelists, John, surnamed son of thunder, at a very advanced age... dictated his Gospel... to his own disciple, the virtuous Papias of Hierapolis..." (*Patrologiae Graeca,* Jaques Paul Migne, Parisiis, 1857); "Drawing their inspiration from the great Papias of Hierapolis, *who lived in the company of the Apostle* who leaned on Christ's breast..." (*Ananstasii Abbatis, Sanctae Romanae Ecclesiae Presbiteri et Bibliothecarii, Opera Omnia,* Anastasius of Sinai, accurante J.P. Migne, Lutetiae Parisiorum, Migne 1852; [*Commentary on the Hexaemeron,* 1. *Patrologiae Graeca* LXXXIX, Migne, p. 860]); "Papias, Bishop of Hierapolis, an ocular witness of John..." (*Georgii Monachi Chronicon,* in aedibus B.G. Teubneri, Lipsiae, Parisiorum, 1904; cf. *Chronikon, syntomon ex diaphoron chronographon te kai exegeton synlegen kai syntheom upo Georgiou Monachou tou epikale Hamartolou,* Lipsiae, Parisiorum, 1863); and so forth. It is also noteworthy that Papias' contemporary, the Apostolic Father and Saint, Justin Martyr, also vouches that "a man among us named John, one of Christ's Apostles, received and foretold that the followers of Christ would dwell in Jerusalem for a thousand years, and that afterwards the universal and, in short, everlasting resurrection and judgment would take place" (Dialogue with Trypho, Justin Martyr, Ch. 81, *The Fathers of the Church,* Christian Heritage, 1948, pp. 277-278). What Papias conveyed, therefore, was nothing but the truth according to the Apostolic Tradition. The evidence is quite clear.

Nonetheless, it is still uncertain whether Papias' faithfulness to John's Gospel extends its influence to his other writings as well, comprehensively known as the *Expositions of the Oracles of the Lord.* And it is in these writings that we encounter Papias' statement of a temporal kingdom. The objection forwarded by the historian Eusebius and his followers, that "Papias himself is candid that he did not directly hear of the apostles speak about a millennium nor their disciples, but rather their acquaintances" is too speculative to merit any dogmatic consideration. As we shall see, this presumptuous approach inevitably results in the eventual falsification of those doctrines of the Apostolic Fathers. By labeling those who provided Papias with information as mere "acquaintances", these men have challenged the truthfulness of his accounts and consequently, that of the original and unmodified doctrines on the millennium of the Catholic Church's Apostolic Fathers as well.

Despite Papias' clearly symbolic and mystical expression of a temporal kingdom (utilizing the same genre employed by his mentor, St. John, in his Book of Revelation), some have falsely accused him of malapropism, claiming that he provided the reader with heretical doctrines. Certainly, were one to interpret such early century parchments in a benign and purely literal sense, then one should also include in this anathema the works of St. John the Evangelist, whose genre is deeply couched in the broad imagery typical of the Bible; the poetic author of the Canticle of Canticles; and many other ecclesiastically inspired authors. Taken exclusively at face-value, there is little wonder that such writings on the temporal kingdom have been labeled as heretical.

Still, one fact is indisputable: absolutely no proof is forthcoming which attests that Papias conveyed a millenaristic doctrine which was to be taken literally. Nonetheless, certain theologians have speculatively adopted this notion. And why, one may ask?

Early on, Jewish converts to Christianity ushered in a heretical doctrine known as *Chiliasm:* this heresy is predicated upon the professed belief that Christ would come down to earth to reign *in the flesh* with his saints for *literally 1000 years* amidst *immoderate carnal banquets,* furnished with an amount of meat and drink such as to surpass the measure of credulity itself. While the author of the Epistle of Barnabas clearly states that these early Jewish converts lacked the resources for proper interpretation (the understanding of the exegetical genres of the first Christians), later Christian authors fell into adopting the purely speculative eusebian theory: that Papias' writings on the temporal kingdom were influenced by such Jews (cf. The Letter of Barnabas, Ch. 10): "But how can the Jews understand or comprehend these things? At any rate we, rightly recognizing them, announce the commandments as the Lord intended. For this reason, he circumcised our hearing and hearts that we should understand these things" (Letter of Barnabas, Ch. 10, *The Fathers of the Church,* CIMA Co., NY, 1947, p. 208).

Eusebius, an historian known for his lack of theological refinement, would set the precedent which would exercise an impressive influence over several theologians during the following centuries. In fact, the Catholic Church regards him *not* for his theological import, which is quite poor, but rather for his contributions as an historian: "Despite his outstanding scholarship, Eusebius is *not* one of the great theologians; his lasting work is due to his work as the great *historian..*" (*Patrology,* Berthold Altaner, Herder and Herder, NY, 1961, p. 263).

Some disciples and protagonists of Eusebius' theology on *Chiliasm* and his appropriating it to several Catholic Church Fathers were, to mention a few, Acacius of Caesarea (the leader of the Homoeans), Eusebius of Emesa (a semi-Arian), Gelasius of Caesarea (Eusebius' second successor), Rufinus of Aquileia (translated Eusebius' writings and adapted them), Philip of Side, Philostorgius, Socrates of Constantinople (a Novatian sympathizer), Sozomen, Theodoret of Cyrus, etc.

Eusebius, Church Historian (263—340 A.D.)

Eusebius Pamphilus of Caesarea in Palestine belonged to the pre-Nicene period. He represented the tumultuous Constantinian epoch marked by Christian persecution. This, in turn, contributed to his anti-heretical literary style, in his attempts to assist the Church in its onslaught against the many sprouting heresies. However, despite his bona fide efforts, Eusebius himself became a victim of doctrinal errors and was, in fact, declared by Holy Mother Church a "schismatic". The Church clearly affirms that Eusebius of Caesarea became a follower of subordinatianism; that he held arianistic views during the debates on the Arian heresy; that he took part in the activities against the Nicene Creed and assisted in deposing St. Athanasius (the promoter of Christ's consubstantiality with the Father and of the Divinity of the Holy Spirit; he regarded St. Athanasius' doctrine as Sabellianism); that he attacked Bishop Marcellus of Ancyra, the defender of the Nicene faith in two dogmatic treatises; that he rejected the consubstantiality of the Father with the Son throughout his life; that he regarded the Holy Spirit as a creature(!); and that he condemned the veneration of images of Christ "so that we may not carry about our God in an image, like the pagans" (*Epitome Historiarum,* 471/5, Lipsiac, Teubner 1868; cf. *Historiae* 7,18 Lipsiac Teubner 1887).

The Catholic Church, while regarding his contribution as an *historian,* does not esteem his theology in the least, due primarily to his poor theological prowess. It has been said that historians tend to identify Tradition based on what is accessible from historical documents, thus reducing the content of present-day Tradition to that which can be supported by documentary evidence. Some, then, may oppose progress and adaptation in the name of fidelity to the past. Indeed, the misappropriation of Papias' doctrines to certain Jewish-Christian heresies of the past emerges precisely from such faulty opinion. Some theologians inadvertently adopted Eusebius' speculative approach as an arsenal of argument, being largely influenced by his interpretation of the millennium. Subsequently, these ideologues associated everything and anything that borders on a millennium with *Chiliasm*, resulting in an unhealed breach in the field of eschatology that would remain for a time, like an ubiquitous stricture, attached to the salient word *millennium*.

Since everything revolves around the interpretation of this word, it is obvious that certain theologians have partially stigmatized the Apostolic Tradition dispersed throughout the orthodox writings of the Apostles and the early Church Fathers, through their misappropriation of certain chiliastic doctrines. However unassumingly, they have done this via the age-old phenomenon of misinterpretation. To give one example, consider the common misinterpretation of Papias' statement that there will be on earth the establishment of "Christ's Kingdom where the just will reign" (note: not on *this* earth, but on a transformed earth). This statement has been misunderstood to signify Christ's personal descent to earth in order to roam about freely in full glory, in the flesh and amidst his saints. Clearly, Papias makes *no mention* whatsoever of Christ coming down to reign "in the flesh", but rather speaks of a "kingdom".

Furthermore, St. Jerome refrains from accusing Papias of heresy. It was "Eusebius [the fourth century historian Eusebius who died 80 years before Jerome] who accused Papias of transmitting the heretical doctrine of *Chiliasm* to Irenaeus and other early churchmen" (*New Catholic Encyclopedia*, McGraw-Hill Pub., NY, 1967, Vol. X, p. 979). Jerome, already cognizant of Eusebius' accusatorial position on the matter and its influence on others, simply states that "he [Papias] it is, *so they say*, who originated the Jewish tradition of the millennium... in which our Lord is to reign in the flesh with his saints" (*De Viris Illustribus,* St. Jerome, 18, Sansoni, Firenze 1964, Ed. Vallarsi II, p. 845). By stating "so they say", Jerome makes an emphatic indication of "them" who accuse Papias of heresy, thereby deliberately avoiding any personal accordance with such beliefs. Needless to say, Eusebius, in his attack, dismisses Papias as "a man of very little intelligence" — the Papias whom the Apostles themselves ordained Bishop of Hierapolis, deeming him worthy of the episcopacy! (*The Faith of the Early Fathers*, W.A. Jurgens, Liturgical Press, Collegeville, MN, 1970, p. 294).

Even in acknowledging Eusebius' observation of Papias' fallibilities, no vicious attacks need follow. Eusebius' counterparts, through their "Theology of Shared Speculations", have made Papias and all Church Fathers who hold to his doctrines the butt of their scurrilous satire for the sake of holding a tight rein on what was the accepted opinion (not Tradition) of their day. Moreover, some of them even contended that Jerome sided with the eusebian theory which held that Papias' temporal kingdom consisted solely of carnal and mundane pleasures; however, this posture simply does not correspond to St. Jerome's specific language.

At the outset of his discourse, Papias explicitly describes his dedicated effort at preserving the truth in its entirety. It is true that Papias freely utilized several literary genres, as well as a few common fables popular to the oral tradition of his day; nonetheless, he employed what Origen (185-253/4 A.D.) defines as the *spiritual sense* in his classical exegesis known as the *Hexapla*.

Origen's exegetical labors comprised three series of works: The *Scholia, Commentaries* and *Homilies*. He believed that Scriptures offer the reader three diverse senses that are superimposed upon one another: the *historical sense*; the *moral sense* and the *spiritual* or *allegorical sense*. He also believed that all Sacred Scripture is a great allegory which has to be interpreted, explained and clarified, lest one be left bereft of the sense and meaning which the inspired author sought to convey. Origen maintained that beneath the letter of Scriptures lies a deeper meaning to be uncovered. And history demonstrates that this exegetical method was indeed familiar to all the Fathers, even if not yet in its codified origenian formulation.

In addition to Origen, we also discover Saint Dionysius, the third century Bishop of Alexandria, who wrote commentaries on the Book of Revelation. In order to understand this inspired book, Dionysius, in his work entitled *On the Promises,* gave a mystical interpretation — indicative of Origen's spiritual or allegorical sense — to the Book of Revelation. Hence such symbols as trees, leaves, water, were not to be interpreted literally, but symbolically, intending a deeper hidden meaning. Even the sacred Book of Sirach confirms the importance given to this spiritual sense: "The man who devotes himself to the study of the law of the Most High explores the wisdom of the men of old and occupies himself with prophecies; He treasures discourses of famous men, and goes to the heart of involved sayings; *He studies obscure parables,* and is busied with *the hidden meanings of the sages"* (cf. Sir. 39:1-3).

It is understood that Eusebius' temperament as an historian often led him to reject this deeper and more spiritual sense. In fact, exegetes concur in saying that Eusebius was torn between two tendencies, so much so that his scriptural writings leave an impression of his embarrassment. Due to an oversight in biblical interpretation, coupled with the subsequent misunderstanding of the orthodox teachings of the Fathers on the sacred texts, his speculative style proved to be the model adopted by many future historians. Be that as it may, we need only turn our attention to the Church Father of the Epistle of Barnabas (ostensibly penned by the Apostle Barnabas himself) who addresses the spiritual method of interpreting Scripture through the symbolism of food:

> When Moses said: "You shall not eat swine, nor
> eagle, nor hawk, nor crow, nor any fish which
> has no scales on it" (cf. Lev. 11:7,10,13-15; Dt.
> 14:8,10,12-14), he included three doctrines in
> his meaning. Moreover, he says to them in

Deuteronomy: "And I will lay my commandments as a covenant on this people." So then it is not a commandment of God to abstain from eating these creatures, but Moses spoke spiritually. Accordingly, he mentioned the swine for the following reason: You shall not cling, he means, to men who are like swine... "Nor shalt thou eat the eagle, nor the hawk, nor the crow." He means that thou shalt not live with or become like such men as know not how to provide their food by labor and sweat, but take other people's property in their lawlessness... "Thou shalt not eat," he says, "lamprey nor polypus nor cuttlefish." He means that you should not become like men who are utterly ungodly and already condemned to death, just as these fish alone are accursed and swim in deep water, and do not rise like the others...

Now grasp fully also the teaching about food. Moses says again: "Eat of every animal that divides the hoof and chews the cud." What does he mean? He means that whoever receives food recognizes him who feeds him and, relying upon him, seems to rejoice... But what does "that divideth the hoof" mean? It means that the righteous both walks in the world and looks forward to the holy age. See how well Moses wrote the law. But how can the Jews understand or comprehend these things? At any rate we, rightly recognizing them, announce the commandments as the Lord intended. For this reason he circumcised our hearing and hearts that we should understand these things (Letter of Barnabas, *Ibid.*).

The contents of this epistle in chapters 1-17 emphasize that the "value and importance of the Old Testament directives on sacrifice, circumcision and *food* were meant in a higher, *spiritual sense*... The Jews... had perverted the will of God and understood the fulfillment the Law in the literal sense" (*Patrology, Ibid.*, p. 80). Barnabas then goes on to explain the way in which the *spiritual sense* had been commonly interpreted, and to demonstrate this point recalls the writings of the psalmist and prophet Ezekiel:

> "And he who does these things shall be like a tree which is planted near the running waters, which shall bring forth its fruit in due season. And his leaf shall not fall off..." Notice how he described the water and the Cross together. He [God] means this: Blessed are they who put their hope in the Cross [of Christ] and descend into the water [of baptism]. For He speaks of their reward "in due season"; at that time, He says, I will repay. But now, when He says: "Their leaves shall not fall off," He means that every word which shall come from your mouth in faith and charity shall profit many for conversion and hope. And again another prophet says: "...And there was a river flowing on the right hand, and beautiful trees grew of it, and whoever shall eat of them shall live forever." This means that we go down into the water full of sins and foulness, and we come up bearing fruit in our hearts, fear and hope in Jesus in the Spirit. "And whoever shall eat of them shall live forever." This means: Whoever hears these things spoken and believes shall live forever (Letter of Barnabas, *Ibid.*, Ch. 11, pp. 209-210).

Referring to the spiritual sense in Scripture, the author of the Psalms as well as St. Methodius, further testify to the deeper meaning that underlies the nude and crude letter. Commenting on the deeper meaning of the passage in Leviticus dealing with the Feast of Tabernacles, St. Methodius

24

reprimands the Jewish Christians who employ a purely literal interpretation of the characteristics of God's kingdom on earth. The Scriptures also support St. Methodius' criticism, describing the glory of all creation when Christ will return to renew all things in himself...

> The Jews, who hover about the bare letter of the Scriptures like so-called butterflies about the leaves of vegetables instead of the flowers and fruit as the bee does, understand these words and ordinances to refer to the sort of tabernacles which they build (The Symposium, Methodius, Logos 9, in *Ancient Christian Writers,* The Newman Press, Westminster, MD, Ed. Quasten & Plumpe, 1958, p. 132).

> ...that the mountains may yield their bounty for the people and the hills great abundance... (Ps. 72:3).

> ...He will judge the peoples with fairness. Let the heavens rejoice and earth be glad, let the *sea* and all within it *thunder* praise, let the *land and all it bears rejoice*, all the *trees* of the wood *shout* for joy, at the presence of the Lord for he comes, he comes to rule the earth (cf. Ps. 96:13).

> Let our barns be filled to overflowing with crops of every kind; our sheep increasing by thousands, by tens of thousands in our fields, may our oxen be well fattened... (cf. Ps. 144:13).

> As for you, mountains of Israel, you shall grow branches and bear fruit for my people Israel, for they shall soon return (Ez. 36:8).

The phrase "let the land and all it bears rejoice" refers to all the elements of the earth: the fruits, plants, vegetables, etc. produced thereof. The psalmist captures these elements in full glory, in a state of "rejoicing", reminiscent of the Fathers' doctrines and St. John's Book of Revelation. As God himself foretold of the promised land *"flowing* with milk and honey" which was to refresh, enliven and cheer men's hearts — implying neither hedonistic nor purely carnal pleasures — so Papias' emulates the spiritual genre typical of his day with no harm to the reader, while complementing that of the psalmist and God himself. (cf. Ex. 3:8: "God called out to him from the bush, 'Moses! Moses!'... I have come down to rescue them from the hands of the Egyptians and lead them out of that land into a good and spacious land, a land flowing with milk and honey..." [Ex. 13:5; 33:3; Dt. 6:3; 11:9; Jos. 5:6; Jer. 11:5; Bar. 1:20; Ez. 20:6]).

This method of properly interpreting Scripture is employed by nearly all the Apostolic Fathers and Church Doctors. As further evidence, consider the author of *The Shepherd of Hermas* and his method of interpreting parables, Origen's *Hexapla,* and even early Christian poetry, in whose development we see the first vestiges of the spiritual, mystical or allegorical sense. For instance, in Christian poetry we find that *the Odes of Solomon, the Sibylline Oracles* and even the *Sayings of Sextus* already form the genre that the very first Christians would adopt and purify from all pagan doctrines. In their inscriptions these early Christians would employ "mystical and symbolic genre to conceal its Christian character from the uninitiated." Let us look at a few discovered epitaphs etched upon Christian tombstones and translated into English.

1) And to see a queen with *golden robe and golden shoes*

2) And set before me *for food the fish* from the spring

3) And gave this to friends *to eat, always...*

4) Having *sweet wine* and giving the mixed cup with *bread*

In these cryptic passages, we can see some of the first symbolic usages of terms relating to riches, foods and beverages, and it is obvious that they intended to convey a deeper spiritual significance. To interpret these early inscriptions in a literal sense would be inconsistent with the cultural and literary context of the early Christians (cf. the biblical methods of exegesis: *Sitz im Leben; Formgeschichte; Redaktionsgeschichte*).

In addition, the Epistle of Barnabas, penned about the year 70-79 A.D., is tantamount to the exegetical genre employed by the first Christians, as well as by the first and second century Church Father, Papias. Just as the Book of Revelation is brimming with spiritual expressions couched in mystical language, with everything ranging from the beast with ten horns and three heads to the exact structural dimensions of the heavenly Jerusalem, likewise Papias employed the same method as that of St. John, his mentor. Indeed, when commenting on this very book, Papias adopted an identical mode of expression known in exegesis as the *spiritual sense.*

As a consequence, we can be assured of steadfast obedience to Tradition when approaching Papias' literature on the concept of a *true* millennium. It is noteworthy that both the Greek Fathers and the New Testament writers did not write in classical Greek, but in Koiné — a common, almost colloquial tongue. This language was popular throughout the Hellenistic world from the third century B.C. to the end of ancient Christianity, that is, until the beginning of the sixth century A.D. Indeed, in his description of the New Jerusalem, Papias' mentor, St. John, conveys a style rich in symbolism while evidencing the common use of this language through mind-boggling images:

> The city was square... fifteen hundred miles in length and width and height... it's wall, one hundred and forty-four cubits... it's foundation was decorated with every precious stone; the first course of stones of jasper, the second sapphire, the third chalcedony, the fourth

> emerald, the fifth sardonyx...

St. John proceeds all the way up to the twelfth stone and adds:

> The twelve gates were twelve pearls, each of the
> gates made from a single pearl; and the street of
> the city was pure gold... The tree of life produces
> fruit twelve times a year, once each month; the
> leaves of the trees serve as medicine for the
> nations (cf. Rv. 21:21; 22:2).

St. Anastasius of Sinai (d.700), a Palestinian monk and exegete who fought against the Monophysites, states in plain terms, "The famous Papias of Hierapolis, the disciple of John the Evangelist... *took a spiritualistic view of the passages of Paradise and referred them to Christ's Church*" (Anagogical Considerations on the Hexaemeron, Anastasius of Sinai, *Patrologiae Graeca,* Jacques Paul Migne, Paris, 1857, LXXXIX, p. 860); and Andreas of Caesarea enjoins his readers to hold in high esteem Papias' words on the inspired Book of Revelation: "I do not have to linger on the inspiration of the Book of Revelation, since Saints Gregory and Cyril have borne witness to its genuineness. Furthermore, the ancients Papias, Irenaeus, Methodius and Hippolytus add their testimony on this point" (Cursus Patrologiae, Omnium SS. Patrum Ecclesiasticorum, Archiepiscopi Caesarae Cappadociae, *Commentarius in Joannis Theologi Apocalypsin,* Tomus Unicus, J.P. Migne Editorem, Paris, 1863, Caput II-C, p. 219).

One cannot, therefore, conclude that Papias intended a *literal sense* to his scholarly contribution on the millenary "age to come". For we know that despite certain theologians who have hypothetically appropriated a literal, carnal, earthly and purely hedonistic character to Papias' literature, such theories are mere *speculative* theological opinions. We also have seen that there are many other highly qualified theologians who have vehemently disagreed with such literal interpretations not only of Papias' writings and those of the author of the Epistle of

Barnabas, but with other Church Fathers and Apologists such as St. Justin, St. Irenaeus of Lyons, Tertullian, Methodius of Olympus, Hippolytus, Lactantius, and so forth.

In conclusion, dismissing all possibility of a millennium, predicated on the basis of a speculative and theoretical assessment of the early Church Fathers' writings, is not sound theology. Indeed, it contrasts with early Church Tradition, and by no means affords Catholics the ability to unequivocally dismiss the reality of a "holy age to come" or a *true* millennium (as opposed to the condemned false *millenarianism*).

St. Justin Martyr, Church Father (100/110 — 165 A.D.)

St. Justin Martyr, martyred with six companions in Rome when he was beheaded for the sake of the Christian faith, is considered the most important apologist of the second century. He wrote two Apologies in defense of the Christian religion; *The Dialogue with Trypho;* and other writings that have been preserved only in minor fragments. It is in his long *Dialogue* — a two-day conversation with Trypho, a man of Jewish origin — that St. Justin mentions an era of peace when quoting the Prophet Isaiah. He explains to Trypho the deeper meaning of Scriptures in these words:

> "Sir," Trypho said... "do you really believe that this place Jerusalem shall be rebuilt, and do you actually expect that you Christians will one day congregate there to live joyfully with Christ, together with the patriarchs, the prophets, the saints of our people and those who became proselytes before your Christ arrived?"

> "Trypho," I replied... "I have declared to you earlier that I, *with many others,* feel that such an event will take place. However, I did

29

point out that there are many pure and pious Christians who do not share our opinion [N.B. these "pious Christians" are not to be equated with the Church Fathers, one of whom is St. Justin]. Moreover, I also informed you that there are some who are Christians by name, but in reality are godless and impious heretics whose doctrines are entirely blasphemous... If you ever encountered any so-called Christians who do not admit this doctrine [of the millennium], but dare to blaspheme the God of Abraham... do not consider them to be real Christians... (please take no offense if I speak my mind), but... they are... children of Abraham in name only, paying lip service to God, while their hearts (as God Himself declared) are far from Him. But *I and every other orthodox Christian feel certain that there will be a resurrection of the flesh, followed by a thousand years* in the rebuilt, embellished, and enlarged city of Jerusalem, as was announced by the Prophets Ezekiel, Isaias and others."

These are the words of Isaias concerning the millennium: "For there shall be a new heaven and a new earth, and the former shall not be remembered... but they shall be glad and rejoice in these things, which I create. For, behold, I make Jerusalem a rejoicing, and my people a joy; and I shall rejoice over Jerusalem, and be glad over My people. And the voice of weeping shall no more be heard in her, nor the voice of crying. There shall no more be an infant of days there, nor an old man that shall not fill up his days; for the child shall die a hundred years old... And they shall build houses and inhabit them; and they shall plant vineyards, and eat the fruits of them, and drink the wine... For as the days of the tree of life, so shall be the days of My people, and the works of their hands shall be multiplied. My elect shall not labor in vain, nor bring forth children for a curse; for they shall be a righteous seed blessed by the Lord, and their posterity with them. And it shall come to pass that before they call, I will hear... Then the wolves and lambs shall feed together, and the lion shall eat like the ox, and the serpent shall eat earth like bread. They shall not hurt nor destroy on my holy mountain, saith the Lord..." (cf. Is. 65:17-25). Now... we understand that **a period of one thousand years is indicated in symbolic language.** When it was said of Adam that "in the day that he eateth of the tree, in that he shall die," we knew he was not a thousand years old [Adam lived to be 963]. We also believe that the words, "The day of the Lord is a thousand years," also led some to the same conclusion. Moreover, **a man among us named John, one of Christ's Apostles, received and foretold that the followers of Christ would dwell in Jerusalem for a thousand years, and that *afterwards* the universal and, in short, everlasting resurrection and judgment would take place. To this our Lord himself testified when He said: "They shall neither marry, nor be given in marriage, but shall be equal to the angels, being sons of God, that is of the resurrection"** (Dialogue with Trypho, *Ibid.*, pp. 277-278). *Note: Justin Martyr's language following the word "afterwards" refers to the New Jerusalem, and not to the millennium.*

In this discussion which took place at Ephesus, St. Justin impresses upon Trypho the necessity of holding fast to the Apostolic Tradition as was passed on from the Apostles to their disciples. He stresses the traditional stance on the millennium based upon the inspired prophet Isaiah and St. John the Apostle. And as Justin was born just one generation after the Apostles, his testimony, like that of Papias (the disciple of St. John), is significant for its orthodoxy and unmodified influence.

St. Irenaeus of Lyons, Church Father (140 — 202 A.D.)

This apostolic witness and doctrinal orthodoxy is further exemplified in the writings of the illustrious and renowned "Father of Catholic Dogmatics", St. Irenaeus of Lyons. St. Irenaeus was schooled in his youth by St. Polycarp of Smyrna (69 — 156 A.D.), the Apostolic Father who saw and listened to the Apostle John, and was later consecrated Bishop of Smyrna by John. Reared with a solid education as his foundation, Irenaeus penned what would become one of the greatest of all refutations, *Adversus Haereses.*

This masterly work against the gnostic heresy is divided into two principal parts. The second part contains five books, the last of which addresses the doctrines surrounding the temporal kingdom. Like his predecessors, including St. John the Apostle, Irenaeus avails himself of the literary genre of his day, the *spiritual sense.* The same truths pronounced by his predecessors come to light as he comments on Sacred Scripture:

> So, the blessing foretold undoubtedly refers to the time of His Kingdom, when the just will rule on rising from the dead; when creation, reborn and freed from bondage, will yield an abundance of food of all kinds from the heaven's dew and the fertility of the earth, just as the seniors recall. Those who saw John, the Lord's disciple, [tell us] that they heard from him how the Lord taught and spoke about these times... Days will come when vines will grow *each with*

ten thousand shoots, and on each shoot *ten thousand* branches, and on each branch *ten thousand* twigs... *ten thousand* clusters... *ten thousand* grains... And other fruits and seeds, and grass... And all the animals who use the products of the soil will be at peace and in harmony with one another, completely at man's beck and call (Adversus Haereses, *Ibid.*).

It is noteworthy that the expression "ten thousand" is often employed by the sacred writers. Indeed, we repeatedly come across references to "ten thousand" to indicate an impressive number, comparable to our modern-day, colloquial expression of "a zillion" — *not,* however, to be taken literally! In any event, Irenaeus employs the same expressions as his predecessors, and Sacred Scripture itself contains similar expressions of the same numerical significance. For example, the psalmist and the sacred author of the Books of Samuel writes:

Let our barns be filled to overflowing with crops of every kind; our sheep increasing by thousands, by *tens of thousands* in our fields, may our oxen be well fattened... (cf. Ps. 144:13).

The chariots of God were *ten thousand;* thousands of them that rejoice (cf. Ps. 68:18).

The woman played and sang: "Saul has slain his thousands, and David his *ten thousands"* (cf. 1 Sm. 18:7; 21:11).

Irenaeus' use of a spiritual sense in this work is evidenced in the early annals of one of the Church's greatest exegetes, Archbishop Andrew of Caesarea. Endowed with extraordinary wisdom and learning, Andrew was capable of penetrating the deeper meaning of Scripture, from which arose his famous hermeneutic works. Andrew gives a spiritual exegesis in the most acclaimed of these works which comments on the Book of Revelation.

This scholarly Archbishop states in his *Preface of the Apocalypse:* "I do not think to linger any more on the inspiration of the Book of Revelation, since Saints Gregory and Cyril have born witness to its genuineness. In addition, the ancients Papias, Irenaeus, Methodius and Hippolytus add their testimony on this point" (*Preface of the Apocalypse, Ibid.*). It appears quite obvious that if this eminent Archbishop had regarded the interpretations of either Papias, Irenaeus or Hippolytus as chiliastic or heretical, he certainly would not have recommended them to anyone for the orthodox interpretation of the Book of Revelation, which is completely couched in mystical and symbolic language. But because *he knew* of the literary genre employed by the Apostolic Fathers, Andrew of Caesarea recommended them for the correct doctrinal interpretation of this inspired book. Indeed, several other scholars have added their approval and endorsements to that of this sixth century scholar and chronicler Archbishop.

NICENE FATHERS

Tertullian, Church Father (155 — 240 A.D.)

"On the whole... his interests were scholarly rather than *speculative*. Tertullian, it is said, may very well have been the most learned man of his day. This was certainly the opinion of St. Jerome, a man of immense erudition himself..." (*New Catholic Encyclopedia, Ibid.*, Vol. XIII, p. 1021). It is noteworthy that Tertullian, unlike the many speculative theologians influenced by Eusebius' poor theology, sticks to the facts. His dissertation on the millennium perfectly agrees with that of his predecessors. In his treatise *Against Marcion,* he addresses the issue:

We do confess that a kingdom is promised to us upon the earth, although before heaven, only in another state of existence; inasmuch as it will be after the resurrection for a thousand years in the divinely-built city of Jerusalem... We say that *this city has been provided by God for receiving the saints on their resurrection, and refreshing them with the abundance of all really spiritual blessings,* as a recompense for those which in the world we have either despised or lost... Of the heavenly kingdom this is the process. *After its thousand years are over, within which period is completed the resurrection of the saints, who rise sooner or later according to their deserts [merits], there will ensue the destruction of the world* and the conflagration of all things at the judgment: we shall then be changed in a moment into the substance of angels, even by the investiture of an incorruptible nature, and so be removed to that kingdom in Heaven [the New Jerusalem] (Adversus Marcion, Tertullian, *Ante-Nicene Fathers,* Henrickson Pub., Peabody, MA, 1995, Vol. 3, pp. 342-343).

And in his work entitled the *Apology,* he clearly shows the two stages of the kingdom of God: first a millennium, followed by the definitive kingdom in which the human race will be raised forever:

When, therefore, the boundary and limit, *that millennial interspace,* has passed when even the outward fashion of the world itself... passes away, then the whole human race shall be raised again, to have its dues meted out according as it has merited in the period of good or evil, and thereafter to have these paid out through the immeasurable ages of eternity... But the profane... in like manner shall be consigned to the punishment of everlasting fire (Apologia del Cristianesimo, Tertullian, *Ante-Nicene Fathers,*

Henrickson Pub., Peabody, MA, 1995, Vol. 3, pp. 53-54).

At this point, we begin to see the first characteristics of what the kingdom of God on earth will be like. From the writings of the aforementioned Church Fathers, this temporal kingdom appears to be an "age", commonly known as a thousand years (signifying a period of time), in which God's elect or saints will reign in perfect accord with God's Will. Furthermore, all creation will rejoice such that all humans, animals, plants, trees, fruits, etc. will not only abound in virtue of the divine fecundity of almighty God's blessing, but also abide in perfect harmony. This "divine fecundity" is not to be taken in the carnal sense as, for example, the sheer propagation in quantity, but in a divine and spiritual sense, according to good pleasure of the Lord who "fills the earth with his glory."

Hippolytus of Rome, Church Father (d.235 A.D.)

Another Church Father and scholar is the Bishop and Greek author, Hippolytus of Rome. A reputed disciple of Irenaeus and contemporary of Origen, Hippolytus was no stranger to the exegetes and rhetoricians of his day. Assimilating their literary genre into that of his own, he candidly expresses the economy of salvation in a nutshell. In his brilliant exegetical work entitled the *Chronicle,* preserved only in part, he advises his listeners not to be hasty of the day of Judgment nor of the millennium; the end of the world (as we know it) would come only after six thousand years, and was, therefore, still far off (cf. *New Catholic Encyclopedia, Ibid.,* Vol. VI, p. 1140).

EARLY ECCLESIASTICAL WRITERS

St. Methodius of Olympus, Ecclesiastical Writer (+300 A.D.)

St. Methodius of Olympus, a reputed bishop and martyr, was the third century Greek author of several famous Christian tractates. In his Symposium, Methodius speaks of the eight ages of the world: "Five are the ages of the old law, the sixth age is designated to the Church, the seventh is the millennium of rest [when Christ will reign over the earth], and the eighth designates the eternity of heaven" (*New Catholic Encyclopedia, Ibid.*, Vol. IX, p. 742).

Lactantius, Ecclesiastical Apologist (250—317 A.D.)

A teacher of Latin rhetoric and ever faithful to Christ's Gospel, L. Caecilius Firmianus Lactantius is known for his mastery of form and steadfast witness during the time of the Christian persecutions. Coined the "Christian Cicero" due to the nature of his fluent and sublime language, Lactantius composed seven books, the last of which treats the Last Things. This book, *The Divine Institutes,* brilliantly elucidates the duration of the world which is to last for six thousand years. In keeping with the Apostolic Tradition, Lactantius expounds on the sequence of events that have yet to transpire. He states that at the end of the six thousandth year of the world's existence, there will arise the great rebellion of the lawless one, whom the Fathers identify as the personification of Antichrist. While Scripture is explicit that Antichrist is the spirit of rebellion against God (1 Jn. 2:22; 4:2-3; 2 Jn. 1:7), several of its books state a personification of this spirit (Daniel, Pauline Epistles, Revelation), and whom the Fathers call the lawless one, the contriver, and so forth.

Then, after Antichrist's defeat, the millennium will commence, where Christ will be engaged among his saints. As portrayed in St. John's Book of Revelation, at the end of the thousand years the godless one will arise once more, for one final and terrible battle, followed by the Final Judgment. Lactantius writes in chapters 14 and 24:

> Since all the works of God were completed in six days, the world must continue in its present state through six ages, that is, six thousand years. For the great Day of God is limited by a circle of a thousand years, as the prophet shows, who says: "In Thy sight, O Lord, a thousand years are as one day" (Ps. 89:4). And as God labored during those six days in creating such great works, so His religion and truth must labor during these six thousand years, while wickedness prevails and bears rule. And again, since God, having finished His works, rested on the seventh day and blessed it, at the end of the six thousandth year all wickedness must be abolished from the earth, and *righteousness reign for a thousand years;* and there must be tranquility and rest from the labors which the world now long has endured (The Divine Institutes, Lactantius, *Ante-Nicene Fathers,* Henrickson Pub., Peabody, MA, 1995, Vol. 7, p. 211).

> Therefore, the Son of the most high and mighty God shall come... But He, when He shall have destroyed unrighteousness, and executed His great judgment, and shall have recalled to life the righteous, who have lived from the beginning, *will be engaged among men a thousand years, and will rule them with most just command*... Then they who shall be alive in their bodies shall not die, but during those thousand years shall produce an infinite multitude, and their offspring shall be holy and beloved by God... About the same time also the

prince of devils, who is the contriver of all evils, shall be bound with chains, and shall be imprisoned during the thousand years of the heavenly rule in which righteousness shall reign in the world, so that he may contrive no evil against the people of God. After his coming the righteous shall be collected from all the earth, and, the judgment being completed, the sacred city shall be planted in the middle of the earth, in which God Himself the builder may dwell together with the righteous, bearing rule in it... the sun will become seven times brighter than it is now; the earth will open its fruitfulness and bring forth most abundant fruits of its own accord; the rocky mountains shall drip with honey; streams of wine shall run down, and rivers flow with milk; in short the world itself shall rejoice, and all nature exult, being rescued and set free from the dominion of evil and impiety, and guilt and error. Throughout this time beasts shall not be nourished by blood, nor birds by prey; but all things shall be peaceful and tranquil. Before the end of the thousand years the devil shall be loosed afresh and shall assemble all the pagan nations to make war against the holy city. He shall besiege and surround it. "Then the last anger of God shall come upon the nations, and shall utterly destroy them" and the world shall go down in a great conflagration. The people of God will be concealed in the caves of the earth during the three days of destruction, until the anger of God against the nations and the last judgment shall be ended. "Then the righteous shall go forth from their hiding places, and shall find all things covered with carcasses and bones... But *when the thousand years shall be completed, the world shall be renewed by God,* and the heavens shall be folded together, and the earth shall be changed, and God shall transform men into the similitude of angels, and they shall be white as snow; and they shall always be employed in the sight of the Almighty, and shall make offerings to their Lord, and serve Him forever. At the same time shall take place that second and public resurrection of all, in which the unrighteous shall be raised to everlasting punishments" (*Ibid.*, Vol. 7).

Here we have what is perhaps the finest exposition on the millennium as developed within the Apostolic Tradition. In it, not only do we envision the nature of the foretold "era of peace", but we are presented with the unfolding of eschatological events. It is noteworthy that the expression *"He [Christ] will be engaged among men a thousand years"* does not refer to Christ's carnal reign in the flesh but to his universal reign in the Eucharist: "All the nations you have made shall come to bow before you, Lord, and give honor to your name" (Ps. 86:9). This, as shall be observed, is clearly evidenced in the doctrines of the Fathers and ecclesiastical writers.

Lactantius' genius recapitulates the doctrinal orthodoxy of the temporal kingdom in two paragraphs. Listed in sequence are the world's future events as the Apostolic Tradition would have them unfold. Since two tribulations and two judgments are mentioned, a review of our understanding of "judgment" merits attention. It is quite clear in Scripture — as shall be examined in the succeeding chapter — that the General Judgment is marked by two instances: one, which precedes the era of peace, pertains to all the evildoers who are alive; the other primarily involves all those who have already died but have yet to be reunited to their bodies. It is noteworthy that the General Judgment is not completely separated from the Particular Judgment, but rather a confirmation of it. Although they may be thought of as two judgments in terms of their nature — one private, the other public — they really comprise one single judgment inasmuch as the General corporeally confirms the Particular.

It is a simple fact that the Church teaches of a Last Judgment whose sentences will not be isolated from those of the Particular: "The Last Judgment will hold no surprises for us, as far as our own fate is concerned. We shall have already undergone our own Particular Judgment; our souls already will be in heaven or hell. The purpose of the Last Judgment is primarily to give glory to God... whose wisdom and power, love and mercy and justice have been at work through the whole of life" (*The Faith Explained,* Leo John Trese, Fides Pub. Assn., Chicago, IL, 1959, pp. 183-184); "This General Judgment is already begun at death... We cannot speak of a time, in our sense, between death — the Particular Judgment — and judgment on the Last Day (the General Judgment). We simply cannot know how this can be [outside of time]..." (*A New Catechism —Catholic Faith for Adults,* Herder and Herder, NY, 1969, p. 480).

When speaking of the General Judgment, the Council of Trent mentions three principal signs that shall precede it: a) a defection from the faith, b) the coming of Antichrist, c) the preaching of the Gospel throughout the world. "'This Gospel of the kingdom,' says the Lord, 'shall be preached in the whole world, for a testimony to all nations, and *then* shall come the consummation'" (*Catechism of the Council of Trent,* Christian Press Co., NY, 1905, p. 64). If the Gospel is to become a testimony to all nations (the conversion of all nations, Mk. 13:9-10) before the consummation of the world, then it is quite plausible that there should exist what the Church Fathers define as a temporal kingdom where justice, peace and harmony abide —in short, the conversion of all nations.

Lactantius reiterates the teaching of the Council of Trent when placing the appearance of Antichrist before the conversion of all nations. This, he says, will be followed by the consummation of the world, and the birth of the New heavens and the New earth: "The prince of devils, who is the contriver of all evils, shall be bound with chains, and shall be imprisoned during the thousand years of the heavenly rule in which righteousness shall reign in the world, so that he may contrive no evil against the people of God... When the thousand years shall be completed, the world shall be **renewed** by God" (The Divine Institutes, *Ibid.*).

Another characteristic that emerges from Lactantius' traditional development of the temporal kingdom is the spiritual (not corporeal) reign of Christ on earth. This is not to be confounded with the heresy of *spiritual* or *modified millenarianism,* as shall be discussed at length. The traits of the temporal kingdom described by the Catholic Church Fathers combined with the doctrinal developments of ecclesiastical writers will be the focus of this second section of our thesis. Their ancient writings and understanding of eschatological events will provide us with the resources necessary whereby we may make a comparative study of their doctrines on the millennium with those of the *Chiliasts.*

APOSTOLIC TRADITION

As we have seen, notwithstanding the Apostolic Tradition on the millennium, certain writers have adopted an opaque and unilateral approach in their endeavor to completely dismiss the possibility of a millennium of Christian springtime. This approach, it must be said, is not completely unreasonable. Eusebius of Caesarea, a respected historian of the Church but lacking erudition in matters of biblical exegesis and theology, made no small impact on the scholars of succeeding centuries. We, therefore, find ourselves in need of an in-depth analysis of the Apostolic Fathers' doctrines. This source of Tradition reveals a keynote in determining the authenticity of the unmodified teachings on the millennium handed down from the

Apostles to the present day corpus of Catholic believers, who pledge unconditional obedience to the Church's Magisterium.

Indeed, Cardinal Joseph Ratzinger, the Prefect of the Sacred Congregation for the Doctrine of Faith, made a noteworthy pronouncement in recognizing that the issue of an age to come before the final return of Christ is not yet concluded. A few years ago, Fr. Martino Penasa, an eminent theologian, presented this eschatological matter of Christ's millenary reign (not *millenarianism*) to the Cardinal, who reassured him that the matter is still open to discussion: *"Giacchè la Santa Sede non si è ancora pronunciata in modo definitivo"* [the Holy See has not yet made any definitive pronouncement in this regard] (È imminente una nuova era di vita cristiana?, Padre Martino Penasa, *Il Segno del Soprannaturale,* Udine, Italia, n. 30, p. 10, Ott. 1990). What the Holy See has definitively pronounced is an anathema against a "false" millennium, known as *millenarianism:* a heresy accepted by some who professed a belief in a *carnal* and *visible* reign of Christ for a period lasting literally one thousand years. These erroneous doctrines were indeed rejected.

However, we must emphasize that never has the Holy See condemned the Apostolic Fathers' Tradition in this regard. This is because Tradition finds its roots in the very writings of these Apostolic Fathers whose theological import has enriched the Church for centuries in her Councils, in her documents, and in all that pertains to her doctrine. This deposit of faith, preserved and guarded by the Holy Spirit, has undergone a veritable development throughout the centuries. Entrusted by our Lord to the Apostles to pass on through the twofold light of revelation and inspiration, this divine deposit was, in turn, entrusted by them to their disciples, through the Holy Spirit's guidance: "O Timothy, guard what has been entrusted to you... Guard this rich trust with the help of the Holy Spirit that dwells within us... And what you have heard through many witnesses, entrust to the faithful people who will have the ability to teach others as well... Reflect on what I am saying, for the Lord will give you understanding in everything" (1 Tm. 6:20; 2 Tm. 1:14; 2 Tm 2:7).

When this deposit of the Apostles was passed on to their own disciples, through their oral preaching (kèrygma) and written word, a change occurred in the order of priority: no longer were the Apostles the sole authoritative bearers of the good news, but their disciples were as well. This continuance of the Tradition of the Apostles is summed up in St. Vincent of Lérins' *Commonitory* where he says that:

> If God wished to preserve publicly throughout the ages without change the original meaning of the revealed deposit, oral as well as written, there was only one way to do this: it was to accompany publicly throughout the ages the revealed deposit with an interpretation which had God's help. This he has done. When Christ sent the eleven into the world he told them: All authority in heaven and on earth has been given to me; you, therefore, must go out, making disciples of all nations... and behold I am with you all through the days that are coming... [Mt. 28:19] (Commonitory of 434, Vincent of Lérins, *Patrology,* Johannes Quasten, Spectrum Pub., Utrecht—Brussels, 1850, Vol. I, Ch. 41, pp. 9-10).

Given this promise of Christ, one must seriously ask: Is it possible that God, who has guaranteed the permanence of this divine deposit which he himself had sown in the hearts and minds of his Apostles, should allow that their disciples be totally and unanimously aloof to the teachings on the temporal kingdom of God? This deposit, as we have seen, has both Christ's firm guarantee of guidance in the truth from one generation to the next, and the enduring assistance of his Spirit: "I have much to tell you, but you cannot bear it now. But when he comes, the Spirit of truth, he will guide you to all truth... And he will declare to you the *things that are coming"* (Jn. 16:13). To hold to the erroneous notion of misguidance on the part of such renowned Fathers as Papias, St. Justin Martyr, St. Irenaeus, Tertullian, etc. is to denigrate the authority of the Fathers' doctrines which consistently complement one another. Such unanimity bears witness to the Spirit's divine deposit concerning "things that are coming".

Also, given the fact that Cardinal Joseph Ratzinger himself declared that "the Holy See has not yet made any definitive pronouncement" with regard to an era of peace or an age to come before the end of human history, we are left with the reality of this Tradition on the millennium. St. Vincent, in his *Commonitory of 434,* addresses the most prudent way to respond to situations in which no statement has yet been definitively pronounced by the Church:

> If some new question should arise on which no such decision has been given, they should then have recourse to the opinions of the Holy Fathers, of those, at least, who, each in his own time and place, remaining in the unity of communion and the faith, were accepted as approved Masters; and whatsoever these may be found to have held, with one mind and one consent, this ought to be accounted the true and Catholic doctrine of the Church, without any doubt or scruple (Commonitory of 434, *Ibid.,* pp. 9-10).

> Nothing ought to be believed by posterity save what the sacred antiquity of the Holy Fathers consentient in Christ has held (*Ibid.,* Ch. 43).

In light of this wise counsel, that is, remaining faithful to the Apostolic Tradition when no definitive pronouncement has been made by the Church, we see the reality of a temporal kingdom beginning to take shape. More recently, shortly before the Second Vatican Council this possibility appeared more pronounced than ever. Through her ordinary Magisterium, the

Church consistently taught, as she continues to do, that it is not contrary to Catholic teaching to believe or profess "a hope in some mighty triumph of Christ here on earth before the final consummation of all things. *Such an occurrence is not excluded, is not impossible,* it is not all certain that there will not be a prolonged period of triumphant Christianity before the end" (*The Teaching of the Catholic Church: A Summary of Catholic Doctrine,* Burns Oates & Washbourne, London, 1952, p. 1140).

Since the Church has assumed, on the one hand, an inexorable stance in condemning the doctrines of *Chiliasm* or *millenarianism,* while legitimizing the possibility of an intermediary reign of Christ on the other, she wisely sets forth the crucial distinctions of the good and bad doctrines concerning the millennium. She presents us with an additional source in the formulation of doctrine that seconds her Magisterial teachings, namely the Apostolic Tradition. It is this Tradition which provides us with the confirmation of the existence of a temporal kingdom based upon the principle of unanimous reliability which the Apostolic Fathers enjoy.

Cardinal John Henry Newman describes this unanimity or consensus amongst the Fathers. In his work entitled *Discussions and Arguments on Various Subjects,* Cardinal Newman, like St. Vincent, stresses the importance of this Apostolic Tradition:

> I follow the ancient Fathers... When they speak of doctrines, they speak of them as being universally held. They are witnesses to the fact of these doctrines having been received, not here or there, but everywhere... There is an obvious obligation, indeed, upon the ignorant to submit to those who are better informed... As regards the primitive (Apostolic) Fathers, they do not speak of their own private opinion; they do not say, "this is true, because we see it in Scripture"

— about which there might be differences in judgment — but, "this is true, because in matter of fact it is held, and has ever been held, by all the Churches, down to our times, without interruption, ever since the Apostles..." (*Discussions and Arguments on Various Subjects,* John Henry Newman, Basil Montagu Pickering, London, 1872, II, 1).

Indeed, the Apostolic Fathers themselves — Papias and St. Justin Martyr, for instance — bear witness to the orthodoxy of their unmodified doctrines handed on to them from the Apostles. St. Justin emphasizes the unanimity of the teachings regarding the temporary kingdom prevalent amongst those true Christians who hold fast to the true faith; Papias guarantees that he has not held back a single thing he has "carefully remembered" in this regard:

> If you ever encountered any so-called Christians who do not admit this doctrine [of the millennium], but dare to blaspheme the God of Abraham... do not consider them to be real Christians... (please take no offense if I speak my mind), but... they are... children of Abraham in name only, paying lip service to God, while their hearts (as God Himself declared) are far from Him. But I and *every other orthodox Christian* feel certain that there will be a resurrection of the flesh, followed by a thousand years in the rebuilt, embellished, and enlarged city of Jerusalem, as was announced by the Prophets Ezekiel, Isaias *and others* (Dialogue with Trypho, *Ibid.*).

> So far as you are concerned, I shall not hold back a single thing I carefully learned from *my seniors* and carefully remember, and shall thoroughly guarantee the truth of these matters.

> For I do not delight in wordy accounts, as many people do, but in accounts that tell the truth. Furthermore, I do not take delight in the commandments of anybody else, but in *those* mentioned as having been given by the Lord for our belief and which proceed from Truth itself" (The Fragments of Papias, *Ibid.*).

And should anyone think that these "seniors" mentioned by Papias do not include any of the Apostles, he need only review the following statements: "Papias by name, of Hierapolis, a disciple dear to John... copied the Gospel *faithfully under John's dictation*" (*Codex Vaticanus Alexandrinus, Ibid.*); "The last of these Evangelists, John, surnamed son of thunder, at a very advanced age... dictated his Gospel... to his own disciple, the virtuous Papias of Hierapolis..." (*Patrologiae Graeca, Ibid.*); "Drawing their inspiration from the great Papias of Hierapolis, who lived in the company of the Apostle who leaned on Christ's breast..." (Anagogical Considerations on the Hexaemeron, *Ibid.*); "Papias, Bishop of Hierapolis, an ocular witness of John..." (*Georgii Monachi Chronicon, Ibid.*); etc.

Holy Mother Church, wise as she is, gives the final brush stroke to the canvas of this noble Tradition waxing eloquent in the medium of her ordinary Magisterium:

> There exists the *Tradition of the Apostles,* continued in the Church and impossible to separate from the Church's Tradition, developed through the centuries by the Councils, the Fathers, the liturgy and institutions, the teaching of the Magisterium and of the Doctors, the practice of the faithful and the entire exercise of the Christian life... and that all the truths necessary for salvation are contained in the canonical Scriptures... There is no doctrine of the Church based solely on Scripture

independently of Tradition... (*The Meaning of Tradition*, Yves Congar, Hawthorn Books, NY, 1964, pp. 99-100).

To ensure that the Gospel might remain always alive and whole within the Church, the apostles left Bishops [i.e., Papias, Irenaeus, etc.] as their successors, and made over to them their own position of responsibility as teachers. What was *handed on* by the apostles comprises all that makes for holy living among God's people and the increase of their faith...The tradition *received* from the Apostles develops within the Church under the guiding presence of the Holy Spirit... *The writings of the Holy Fathers of the Church testify* to the life-giving presence of this tradition, as its riches flow into the life and practice of the Church, in its belief and in its prayer. Through the *same* tradition the complete canon of the sacred books is made known, and Holy Scripture itself is understood in greater depth and becomes continuously alive and active... (*Dei Verbum*, Vatican Council II, Costello Pub. Co., Northport, NY, Rev. Ed., 1988, nn. 7-8).

In summary, the Church Fathers' sources have undoubtedly played an integral role in the valid assessment of the apostolic doctrines. Their theological tractates together with Sacred Scripture have consistently received thorough endorsements by the holy and living Magisterium, who alone is privy to their sometimes hidden significance and correct interpretation couched in cryptic language. Thus, for anyone to assume the role of interpreting such texts of his or her own accord would be to go beyond the breach of obedience to that corpus of lawful authority whom God has ordained to guide his Church to the truth in all things. Based upon the unanimity of the Church Fathers' doctrines on the temporal kingdom, not false *millenarianism,* one may support their writings as a central component of that deposit of Catholic faith in what was commonly held to be the doctrine of the Apostles.

Still, we cannot fail to mention the inexorable stance the Church has consistently assumed with regard to the more popular notion of *millenarianism.* Throughout the centuries, the Catholic Church has systematically opposed all false notions of a millennium that speak of Christ's elect reveling in immoderate carnal banquets for the duration of one thousand years. What this millenaristic heresy entails and how it differs from the doctrines of the early Fathers shall be discussed in detail in our next chapter. Since we have thus far only envisioned but a few of the characteristics of the temporal kingdom as contained in the writings of the Fathers, a comparative study of the scholarship of Church Doctors will aid us in acquiring a broader vision of the Church's current stance in this regard.

As we embark upon the scholarship of several eminent Doctors, we must bear in mind the one common thread that joins the teachings of the Apostles with those of the Fathers and Doctors: the holy and living Magisterium of the Catholic Church. This divine office, through which the Holy Spirit principally guides the Church to the truth in all things, pronounces the final word on matters of morals and faith. The Spirit, upon whom the Magisterium depends for proper guidance in all things, provides the faithful with traditional scholarship of orthodox teachers in order to nourish the intellect with divine understanding.

Therefore, in our presentation of the teachings of certain notable Doctors on the Last Things, we will incorporate in this coming chapter those issued statements that proceed from her Magisterium as well.

CHAPTER 3

THE CHURCH DOCTORS SPEAK

St. Augustine of Hippo, Church Doctor (354 — 430 A.D.)

At the outset of our presentation of the Church Fathers, we simply touched upon the distinction between them and the Church Doctors. By presenting here certain notable Doctors who have penetrated Scripture to such an extent that they extraordinarily enriched the Church in her understanding of the Sacred Writ, we will more readily perceive the Apostolic Tradition's development in the succeeding centuries of Christian orthodoxy. The theology of such Doctors as St. Augustine, St. Bernard, St. Thomas Aquinas and St. Robert Bellarmine shares one common thread that runs throughout their writings: orthodoxy.

The Church Doctor and Bishop of Hippo, St. Augustine (*Doctor gratiae*) has been quoted as being opposed to the concept of a temporary kingdom that implies a millennium. This is only correct, however, when understood according to the era in which he lived; that is, he opposed the prevalent perception of the millenary kingdom according to the false and perverted notion of *millenarianism*. This is evidenced in his treatise in *De Civitate Dei* in which he dismisses the possibility of a carnal reign of Christ with his saints on earth.

It is worthy of mention that Augustine's writings on the

millennium have been meticulously studied throughout the centuries by scores of renowned theologians. While admitting the complexity and ambiguity of Augustine's writings, these scholars consistently came to different conclusions regarding their interpretations.

Regardless of the various interpretations, it is clear that Augustine in no way condemns the doctrines of the Fathers' temporary kingdom. Through his exposition of the first of what certain theologians consider his four ways, whereby one may interpret the "thousand years" of the Book of Revelation, Augustine concurs, at least in part, with the concept of a millennium:

> 1) Those who, on the strength of this passage [of Revelation 20:1-6], have suspected that **the first resurrection is future and bodily,** have been moved, among other things, specially by the number of a thousand years, as if it were a fit thing that the saints should thus enjoy a kind of **Sabbath-rest during that period, a holy leisure after the labors of six thousand years** since man was created...(and) **there should follow** on the completion of six thousand years, as of six days, **a kind of seventh-day Sabbath in the succeeding thousand years;** and that it is for this purpose the saints rise, viz., to celebrate this Sabbath. **And this opinion would not be objectionable, if it were believed that the joys of the saints, in that Sabbath shall be spiritual, and consequent on the presence of God...** But as they [carnal millenarians] assert that those who then rise again shall enjoy the leisure of immoderate carnal banquets, furnished with an amount of meat and drink such as not only to shock the feeling of the temperate, but even to surpass the measure of credulity itself, such assertions can be believed

only by the carnal. They who believe them are called by the spiritual Chiliasts, which we may reproduce by the name of Millenarians...(*De Civitate Dei [The City of God],* Augustine of Hippo, Catholic University of America Press, Washington, 3rd Printing, 1977, Bk. XX, Ch. 7).

In this first way of interpreting the millennium, Augustine outlines the distinction between what may be considered a valid theory congruent with the doctrines of the Fathers, and the heresy of millenarianism. Although he may be said to confirm the veracity of the apostolic witness by stating that the Sabbath rest may be understood as a "bodily resurrection", for a "period", "a kind of seventh-day Sabbath", and "a thousand years", one may conversely argue on the strength of three other allegorical interpretations he utilizes regarding the end time of the world — that period which extends from the Incarnation to the end of the world as we know it — when, after the Final Judgment of all the dead, God will rest from all his labors in the New Jerusalem for all eternity. Thus, this period of which St. John speaks, in which the saints will undergo a first resurrection and reign with Christ, is to be understood simply as the interval that spans from Christ's Incarnation to his final return in glory and majesty to pronounce the final word upon all history. In fact, this has been precisely the way most have come to interpret Augustine's writings on the millennium: as an allegory represented by an interval of spiritual resurrection of Christians who are now spiritually reigning with Christ both on earth and in heaven and awaiting the day of his final return in glory:

2) The devil, then, is not bound during the whole time which this book [of Revelation] embraces — that is, **from the first coming of Christ to the end of the world** — not bound in this sense, that during this interval, which goes by the name of **a thousand years,** he shall not seduce the Church... (*De Civitate Dei, Ibid.*, Ch. 8).

This way of interpreting the millennium is indeed allegorically valid, but does not explain Augustine's expression of a "period... in the successive thousand years" in which there will take place "a bodily first resurrection"; nor does it dismiss Augustine's other allegorical way in which one might safely interpret the millenary kingdom as the whole duration of the earth. In short, the exclusive adoption of one allegorical way is an exclusion of Augustine's other ways. While never insisting on one way, Augustine offers the reader several allegories:

> He the Apostle saw in the Apocalypse "an Angel coming down from heaven... And he laid hold of the dragon... and bound him a thousand years"... Now the thousand years may be understood in two ways, so far as occurs to me:
>
> 3) because these things happen [the Angel chaining the dragon] in the sixth thousand of years or the sixth millennium (the latter part of which is now passing)... **which is to be followed by a Sabbath which has no evening, the endless rest of the saints,** so that... he calls the last part of the millennium the part that is which had yet to expire before the end of the world — a thousand years...;
>
> 4) or he used the thousand years as an equivalent for **the whole duration of this world**... (*Ibid.,* Ch. 7).

It is also noteworthy that Augustine's writings on the millennium concur with the author of the Letter to the Hebrews who states:

> In reference to the **seventh day,** Scripture somewhere says, "And God rested from all his work on the seventh day"; and again, in the place we have referred to, God says, "They shall never enter into my rest." Therefore, since it

remains for some to enter, and those to whom it was first announced did not because of unbelief, God once more set a day, "today", when long afterward he spoke through David the words we have quoted: "Today, if you should hear his voice, harden not your hearts." Now, if Joshua had led them into the place of rest, God would have not spoken afterward of another day. Therefore, **a Sabbath rest still remains for the people of God.** And he who enters into God's rest, rests from his own work as God did from his. Let us strive to enter into that rest, so that no one may fall, in imitation of the example of Israel's unbelief (cf. Heb. 4:4-11).

Not only does Scripture, the living Word of God, explicitly mention a "Sabbath rest that remains for the people of God," but it even encourages us, the readers, to strive to enter into it! And so that no one may argue that the author of Hebrews intended "today" to mean the days of David, he clarifies its meaning with the following: "Encourage one another *daily, while it is still 'today',* so that no one grows hardened by the deceit of sin... **Therefore, while the promise of entrance into his rest still holds,** we ought to be fearful of disobeying lest any of you be judged to have lost his chance of entering" (cf. Heb. 3:13; 4:1). Clearly, the expression "today" used here does not address the people of David's day, nor for that matter those of the author's own day, as the author makes it quite clear that "it is still today," and that today, therefore, is a "daily" occurrence. "Today" will come to a close only when "we enter into his rest," as the author puts it. And what other rest can this possibly refer to if not that to which Augustine alludes in similar terms — the millennium?

While Augustine's writings share a common thread with Sacred Scripture, they must also endure the scrutiny of expert theologians who, while expressing diverse opinions, attest to the multiplicity of ways in which they may be interpreted.

Indeed, after meticulously studying these writings, renowned theologians have commented on their complexity and ambiguity. In 1956 G. Folliet admitted to having discovered several millenaristic tendencies, however cryptic, in Augustine's doctrines on the millennium as, for example, when he speaks of a "Sabbath" to indicate three distinct periods of the Church's history (*La Typologie du sabbat chez saint Augustin. Son interprétation millenariste entre 389 et 400,* G. Folliet, Revue études Augustiniennes II, 1956, pp. 371-390). In 1986 Martin Dulaey conversely held that such teachings rather demonstrated a purely allegorical nature (*L'Apocalypse, Augustin et Tyconius,* in: *St. Augustine et la Bible,* M. Dulaey, a cura di A.M. la Bonnardière, Paris, 1986, pp. 369-386). In 1993, the subject of millenarianism was revisited by J. Kevin Coyle (Augustine's "Millenarianism" Reconsidered, J. Kevin Coyle, *Augustinus 38,* 1993, pp. 155-164). Coyle based his studies upon the former scholarship of many noted theologians who have studied Augustine's writings on this subject. Despite his rigorous research, Coyle emerged with no startling theological contribution, other than a homogenous presentation of Catholic scholarship on the millennium. In 1995 J. Delumeau simply added a brief reflection on the long-standing debate of Augustine's millenaristic views that continue to prevail even to this day (*Mille ans de bonheur. Une histoire du paradis,* J. Delumeau, Paris, 1995).

In light of the aforementioned quotation, we see that Augustine, having drawn his information from many learned and holy men, in particular the Apostolic Fathers and certain ecclesiastical writers of his day, begins his dissertation on the millennium by stating that which is theologically acceptable and in accord with Church teaching. This is what we have referred to as "the first way". He then goes on to express a personal allegory, when stating "as occurs to me..." In doing so, he denotes a symbolic interpretation of the words of the inspired Book of Revelation. It is noteworthy, however, that the four different ways he presents in relating the concept of a millennium all possess peculiar nuances. They are here laid out in detail:

a)   The first characteristics Augustine attributes to the
     millennium are:

  1)   a first bodily resurrection;

  2)   a period;

  3)   occurring after 6000 years;

  4)   is called "a kind of seventh-day Sabbath";

  5)   lasts for the succeeding 1000 years;

b)   The second group instead bears the following traits:

  1)   from the first coming of Christ to the end of the
       world;

  2)   an interval;

  3)   lasts for 1000 years;

c)   The third group:

  1)   is called "a Sabbath"

  2)   has no evening; is endless;

  3)   is symbolized by 1000 years;

d)   The fourth group:

  1)   the whole duration of the world;

2)   is symbolized by 1000 years.

The first way differs theologically from all others in matters of designation and duration and is called "a kind of seventh-day Sabbath". The others are referred to as "an interval", "a Sabbath". The first way lasts for a period of about 1000 years ("in the succeeding thousand years"), whereas the others for the duration of the Church ("from the first coming of Christ to the end of the world"), of eternity ("the endless rest of the saints"), of the world's existence ("the whole duration of the world").

The third way, as stated, had gained particular momentum due to the influence of a third century historian. Despite Augustine's presentation of the first way, which may be considered an approach to the millennium congruent with the Fathers' doctrines, he also offers other allegorical ways, so it appears, in keeping with the mainstream theology of those thinkers of his day. His nuances bear witness to this, as does the Apostolic Fathers' unanimity to their orthodoxy. What can be said of these four expressions, whether all distinct or partly sharing certain traits, is that the characteristics of all four are in accord with Church teaching. This will become more evident when we treat the ecclesiastical condemnations of *millenarianism* in our next section.

Augustine, in keeping with the Apostolic Tradition, reiterates a version similar to the doctrines contained in the writings of Lactantius which stated, "The world must continue in its present state through six ages, that is, **six thousand years**... At the end of the six thousandth year all wickedness must be abolished from the earth, and righteousness reign for a thousand years," thereby placing the millennium in the **seventh thousandth year**, the day in which God rested from all his labors. (The Divine Institutes, *Ibid.*). This idea of the world enduring for the span of 7000 years as a symbolic reference to the seven days of creation also finds its roots in the writings of an earlier Church Father, the author of the Epistle of Barnabas. Therein, he illustrates the veritable reality of a Sabbath rest.

> Concerning **the Sabbath** He (God) speaks at the beginning of creation: "And God made in six days the works of His hands, and on the seventh day He ended, and rested on it and sanctified it." Note, children, what "He ended in six days" means. It means this: **that the Lord will make an end of everything in six thousand years.** And He Himself is my witness, saying: "Behold the Day of the Lord shall be a thousand years." So, then, children, in six days, that is in six thousand years, everything will be ended. "And He rested on the seventh day." **This means: when His Son will come and destroy the time of the lawless one and judge the godless, and change the sun and the moon and the stars — then He shall indeed rest on the seventh day...** If, then, anyone is able **now** to hallow the day which God sanctified, by being pure in heart, we are completely deceived. See that we shall **then** indeed sanctify it when we enjoy true repose... because we have been made just ourselves and shall have received the promise, when there is no more sin, but all things have been made new by the Lord; then we shall be able to sanctify it, having been made holy ourselves. Furthermore, He says to them: "I will not abide your new moons and your Sabbaths." You see what He means: The present Sabbaths are not acceptable to Me, but that Sabbath which I have made, in which, *after* **giving rest to all things, I will make the beginning of the eighth day, that is, the beginning of another world** (Letter of Barnabas, *Ibid.*, Ch. 15).

Based upon these doctrines it seems evident that at the approximate end of the six thousandth year there will begin what the Fathers call a "seventh day Sabbath", in which God will rest with his saints for a long period of time, known as *a thousand years*. **The Duoay Rheims version of the Holy Bible's chronology puts the creation of Adam and Eve 6,000 years ago or in the year 4000 B.C.** (some Protestant theologians claim 4004 B.C.). This would place us not only on the threshold of the third millennium, but of the end of the times of the reign of the human will and the beginning of the times of the reign of God's Divine Will, or God's rest in creation.

Still, despite Augustine's incorporation of the Apostolic Fathers' doctrines into his own scholarship, it is not certain whether that "period... in the successive thousand years" of which he speaks is congruent with the "period of peace" mentioned in the Fathers' writings. Nor is it altogether clear whether he concurs with the Fathers in their interpretation of the "Sabbath" which precedes the *final resurrection* of all the dead at the end of the world, and which lasts for an approximate "period of a thousand years".

One can speculate endlessly. What really matters is that neither the doctrines of the early Fathers nor those contained in Augustine's allegorical ways have ever been condemned by Holy Mother Church; they are all tenable positions concerning the millennium. What has been condemned is the falsified notion of *millenarianism*. But before we can address this heresy, something needs to be said on the prevalent, reigning attitude diametrically opposed to the feasibility of the Fathers' doctrines on the true millennium.

As we have seen, due to certain eusebian protégés, the second allegorical way of interpreting the millennium became the exclusive way, perhaps to safeguard the faithful from all breaches of faith resulting from erroneous interpretations of the millennium, but with the backlash of having to forfeit those orthodox teachings that have come to us from the Apostles and their disciples. Having gone awry in the exclusive adoption of the allegorical interpretation triggered by Eusebius' poor speculative theological prowess, such theologians have sent the possibility of a "period of rest", an "era of peace" preceding the end of the world, out into the far reaches of space where its glorious terrestrial manifestation alone could bring it back to earth. They had, in effect, not only confused this third century chronicler's recounts of Church *history* with the Fathers' orthodox *theology,* but availed themselves of Augustine's allegorical way in the process. And, needless to say, the sciences of history and theology are quite distinct.

Subsequently, the millennium became exclusively referred to as a mere symbol, an allegorical expression indicating that period in time that spans from the Incarnation of Christ to his final coming in glory. It is, moreover, highly probable that for fear of preaching what might be considered as the condemned heresy of a "false millennium" or "millenarianism", many scholars preferred to reticently avoid discussing any notion of a temporal kingdom rather than engaging in a heated debate on what was an undeniably cryptic heresy. Though the Church had never condemned the Apostolic Fathers' doctrines in this regard, she did in fact condemn "even modified forms of this falsification of the kingdom to come under the name of *millenarianism,* especially the 'intrinsically perverse' political form of *secular messianism"* (*CCC, Ibid.,* 676). Unless a professor or scholar kept abreast of patristic doctrine, he would be at a loss when attempting to engage in debate on the nature surrounding the true and false doctrines of the millennium.

Augustine's allegorical way of interpreting the thousand years provided a convenient and practical solution: it skirted the issue of millenaristic doctrines altogether, while at the same time enjoyed the backing of an eminent Doctor whose writings have been endorsed by the Church for centuries. This allegorical way would thus become the common way — *nota bene:* not the Traditional way — in which many scholars would interpret the thousand years as prophesied in the inspired Book of Revelation.

However, a careful study of Augustine's text reveals that through his presentation of the various ways of interpreting the thousand years he is not, by any means, setting forth an unequivocal dissertation on the millennium: that one way is to prevail over the others. Conversely, it can be gleaned from his writings that his intention is explicit that all ways are valid and equally worthy of respect; that is, they are to be understood as complementary. One way can be correctly understood only if interpreted in light of the others. Because certain scholars have in good faith acquiesced in the exclusive adoption of one of Augustine's ways, they have unassumingly falsified in part the sacred text of St. John's Book of Revelation as interpreted by the Fathers and this eminent Church Doctor.

Augustine's exposition of the four ways clearly contradicts this standard. By providing his readers with several possibilities of interpreting the thousand years, Augustine is availing himself of a literary genre common to biblical exegesis where a sacred text can convey several truths concomitantly. In point of fact, the Apostle Barnabas, in his Epistle, tersely conveys two truths from one noun: "the righteous both walks in the world and looks forward to *the holy age*" (Letter of Barnabas, *Ibid.*).

To further exemplify the impossibility of adopting just one way, we need only turn our attention to the words of Jesus himself. In Matthew's Gospel, he states:

> Do not think that I have come to bring peace upon the earth. I have come to bring not peace but the sword. For I have come to set man against his father, a daughter against her mother, and a daughter-in-law against her mother-in-law; and one's enemies will be those of his household (Mt. 10:34-36).

We know that, by way of his early Father-predecessors, Augustine was well aware of those characteristics pertaining to the thousand year reign of saints, which he called *"a period"*, the *"endless rest of the saints"*, or *"the whole duration of the world"*. Having said this, he would never have intended any of these ways to be exclusive. For the last way treats of this present earth — before its transformation and subsequent renewal — in which there will always be the sword — namely strife, discord, wars and the like. Thus, to treat the last way (the whole duration of the world) as the valid interpretation to the exclusion of all others would only result in a constant begging of the question; the probability of reconciling it with the rest, peace and harmony of the millennium far exceeds the parameters of theology. Hence the need of a timely equilibrium to harmonize the apparent paradoxical qualities of all variations. Only then can we rightly intend our Lord's words... "Holy Father, keep them in your name that you have given me, so that they may be one just as we are one" (Jn. 17:11).

Indeed, Jesus came to bring a sword and sow division upon *this* earth, but by the same token, he nurtured an earnest desire to one day bestow unity not to *this* earth, but to a *"new* earth". This new earth, accompanied by the new heavens, is the missing link that reconciles Augustine's last way with his first way, and that has evaded one-way exponents for centuries.

For the sake of clarifying what we had earlier quoted as the condemned heresy of *millenarianism,* and before proceeding to the doctrines of the great Doctors Bernard of Clairvaux, Thomas Aquinas and Robert Bellarmine, let us turn to the pronouncements of Holy Mother Church. The Church, through the exercise of her ordinary Magisterium, has appropriated certain titles to the various forms of the heresy *millenarianism.* Here we shall present them while keeping in mind the aforementioned doctrines of the holy Church Fathers.

Magisterium and Millenarianism

In order to arrive at a certitude of faith in matters regarding eschatology, in particular a temporal kingdom, we must base our ideas upon the guidance of the Church's universal Magisterium. The Second Vatican Council, in its document *Lumen Gentium*, mentions the twofold magisterial office exercised by the Pope and the Bishops. Present in the Church is her charism of *extraordinary* Magisterium as well as the guidance of her *ordinary*, to which all the faithful are obliged to lend loyal respect (*Lumen Gentium*, n. 25, Vatican Council II, Costello Pub. Co., Northport, NY, Revised Ed., 1988; *CCC, Ibid.*, 2034, 2039). Apropos of her ordinary Magisterium, the false chiliastic concept of *millenarianism* is clearly distinguished from the concept of a temporary kingdom, also known as an *era of peace*, as prophesied by the Blessed Virgin Mary at Fatima. Although it may seem that there are far too many names given to the heresy most commonly known as *millenarianism*, we must keep in mind that they derived from the multiplicity of nuances that ensued throughout the centuries. Such forms containing the same elemental millenaristic doctrines were, nonetheless, gradually condemned one by one. Let us here examine these doctrines and their ecclesiastical anathemas.

Pope Zephyrinus in 217 declared the millenarian doctrines of Montanus to be heretical.

On St. Augustine's authority, the Council of Ephesus (431) condemned belief in millenarianism as a superstitious aberration (*Utopia the Perennial Heresy*, Thomas Steven Molnar, Sheed & Ward, NY, 1967, p. 24).

Augustine had stated the following: "But as they [carnal millenarians] assert that those who then rise again shall enjoy the leisure of immoderate carnal banquets, furnished with an amount of meat and drink such as not only to shock the feeling of the temperate, but even to surpass the measure of credulity itself, such assertions can be believed only by the carnal. They who believe them are called by the spiritual Chiliasts, which we may reproduce by the name of Millenarians..."(*De Civitate Dei, Ibid.*).

Pope Pius XI declared that "the Church has rejected even modified forms of the falsification of the Kingdom to come under the name of millenarianism" (*Gaudium et Spes,* 20-21, Vatican Council II, Costello Pub. Co., Northport, NY, Rev. Ed., 1988; *CCC, Ibid.*, 676 *inter alia)*.

Pope Pius XII and the Holy See stated that millenarianism may not be sustained even in its mild form: "The system of mitigated Millenarianism, which teaches that Christ the Lord will come visibly to this earth to rule..." cannot be safely taught (*Enchiridion Symbolorum, definitionum et declarationum de rebus fidei et morum,* Heinrich Denzinger, 3839, *cura di* Peter Hünermann, Barcinone, Herder Pub., 1965 [ed. Dehoniane Bologna 1995]; *Acta Apostolicae Sedis,* Rome, 1944, ser. 2, Vol. XI, n. 7).

"Spiritual millenarianism" was formally declared as being in opposition to the teachings of the symbols of the faith (*Enchiridion Symbolorum,* Heinrich Denzinger, 423, cura di Johannes B. Umberg SJ, 1951), for in the prospect of Matthew 16:27: *"Filius hominis venturus est **in gloria Patris sui** cum Angelis, tunc reddet unicuique secundum opera sua"* (For the Son of man will come with his Angels **in his Father's glory,** and then he will repay everyone according to his conduct). Christ cannot come in the Father's glory unless with the scope of requiting each individual according to his deeds.

It is very important to note that Spiritual Millenarianism, as shall be discussed, is not to be confused with the "spiritual blessings" that accrue to the temporal kingdom in the doctrines of the early Church Fathers. Holy Mother Church, wise as she is, has systematically listed all formal condemnations of millenarianism, thereby distinguishing them from the orthodox doctrines of the Fathers.

Qu.: *Quid sentiendum de systemate Millenarismi mitigati, docentis scilicet Christum Dominum ante finale iudicium, sive praevia sive non praevia plurium iustorum resurrectione, **visibiliter in hanc terram regnandi** causa esse venturum* [Question: What must one think regarding the system of mitigated Millenarianism, which teaches that Christ the Lord, before the final judgment — whether or not it precedes the resurrection of the majority of the righteous — **will come visibly to reign on this earth?**]

Resp. (*confirmata a Summo Pontifice, 20 lul.*): *Systema Millenarismi mitigati tuto doceri non posse* [Response (confirmed by the Holy Father, 20 July 1944): The system of mitigated Millenarianism cannot be safely taught] (*Enchiridion Symbolorum, Ibid.*, 3839).

Pope Paul VI briefly touched upon the misleading notion of a sensual or carnal millenarianism (*The Christian Faith in the Documents of the Catholic Church*, J. Neuner & J. Dupuis, Harper Collins, London, 1995, n.673).

The Church has rejected even modified forms of this falsification of the kingdom to come under the name of *millenarianism*, especially the "intrinsically perverse" political form of *secular messianism* (*CCC, Ibid.*, 676).

Contained in the ecclesiastical anathemas are several nuances all of which depict an earthly kingdom imbibed with pleasures ranging from the flesh to the spirit. So as to more readily understand these doctrines and in order to come to terms with them, an etymological analysis is in order. We may ask ourselves: What are the millenarian doctrines of Montanus? What is its mild form? What is spiritual millenarianism? What is modified millenarianism? etc. We shall now uncover the answers to these questions.

Millenarianism at its birth was swiftly nipped in the bud. However, at that point it was only a relatively simplistic and conspicuous doctrine: Christ will reign on earth, in the flesh, for a thousand years, and will revel with his saints in immoderate carnal banquets replete with foods and drinks of all imaginable species. This utopian hedonism, informally condemned by the early corpus of faithful Christians, originated amongst the Jewish converts to the Christian faith who, perhaps being accustomed to the dependency of an oral tradition, misinterpreted the words of the Apostolic Fathers:

> But how can *the Jews* understand or comprehend these things? At any rate we, rightly recognizing them, announce the commandments as the Lord intended. For this reason he circumcised our hearing and hearts that we should understand these things (Letter of Barnabas, *Ibid.*).

> For there are also many rebels, idle talkers and deceivers, especially *the Jewish Christians*. It is imperative to silence them, as they are upsetting whole families by teaching for sordid gain what they should not... Therefore, admonish them sharply, so that they may be sound in faith, instead of paying attention to Jewish myths and regulations of people who have repudiated the faith (Ti. 1:10-14).

> Il testo dell'Apocalisse mantiene una grandissima discrezione sulla felicità degli eletti

THE TRIUMPH OF GOD'S KINGDOM

durante il regno di mille anni. Mentre *l'esegesi ebraica e millenarista 'stretta' descrive la felicità paradisiaca in modo fantastico...* [The text of the Apocalypse conveys with utmost discretion the happiness of the elect during the thousand year reign. Whereas the *Hebrew exegesis* and *literal millenarianism* describe such paradisal happiness with bizarre imagery...] (Articolo sul Millenarianismo, *Il Grande Dizionario delle Religione,* Paul Poupard, Cittadella Editrice, Assisi, Italy, 1990, p. 1346).

What is more, the contents of the Epistle of Barnabas, Chapters 1-17, emphasize the "value and importance of the Old Testament" in its hidden and deeper meaning:

God's directives on sacrifice, circumcision and *food* were meant in a higher, spiritual sense... *the Jews...* had perverted the Will of God and understood the fulfillment the Law *in the literal sense* (*Patrology, Ibid.*).

In addition to these texts, we can refer to the famous quotation of the highly acclaimed and ecclesiastically revered Catholic theologian, Jean Daniélou. Here he speaks not only of the erroneous Jewish-Christian infiltration into the orthodox doctrines of the Fathers, but of the traditional truth in chronological order: the millennium — "a period of time", followed by the return of Christ, the resurrection of the dead, the judgment of the dead and the New heavens and New earth. He writes:

Millenarianism, the belief that there will be an earthly reign of the Messiah before the end of time, is the Jewish-Christian doctrine which has aroused and continues to arouse more argument than any other. The reason for this, however, is probably a failure to distinguish between the various elements of the doctrine. On the one hand, it seems hard to deny **that it contains a truth which is a part of the stock of the Christian teaching,** and which occurs in the New Testament in I-II Thessalonians, in I Corinthians, and in the Revelation of John. *This truth* is that of the Parousia, Christ's return to this earth at the end of time to establish his kingdom, a belief which was attacked by Marcion, and which Tertullian rightly defended against him. It *implies* no more than that there is to be **a period of time,** the duration of which is unknown to men, and which in the last days will cover the return of Christ, the resurrection of the saints, the General Judgment, and the inauguration of the New creation (*A History of Early Christian Doctrine Before the Council of Nicea,* Jean Danielou, London, Darton, Longman & Todd, Westminster Press, Philadelphia, PA, 1964, p. 377).

Millenarianism, which the *Ascension* shows to have been present in the Syro-Palestinian area, is an early type, representing a common basic belief, and not connected with any particular group. I-II Thessalonians show that it was the belief of Christians in Greece, since Paul is content merely to add some precision in detail, and assumes that his correspondents were expecting this earthly reign of Christ. Moreover, the doctrine underlies the various developments to be found in the Revelation of John. The essential affirmation is of **an intermediate stage** in which the risen saints are still on earth and have not yet entered their final stage, for this is one of the aspects of the mystery of the last days which has yet to be revealed (*Ibid.*, pp. 377,

379).

The newborn heresy originally known as *Chiliasm* and later as *millenarianism,* having been condemned from the beginning would, nonetheless, assume throughout the centuries certain doctrinal changes and the subsequent titles:

* *Chiliasm*
* *millenarianism*
* *false millenarianism*
* *earthly millenarianism*
* *crass millenarianism*
* *secular millenarianism*
* *radical millenarianism*
* *carnal millenarianism*
* *mitigated millenarianism*
* *modified millenarianism*
* *spiritual millenarianism*
* *a falsified millennium.*

Let us begin with the first heresy commonly known as Chiliasm.

Chiliasm, from the Greek kiliàs (1,000), was the name given to the belief that the 1000 years mentioned in St. John's Book of Revelation is to be taken literally. When Latin began to exercise its influence over the Christian speaking world, Chiliasm became popularly known as *millenarianism,* from Latin *mille* (1,000). It professed the belief in Christ who would come down to earth to reign *in the flesh* with his saints *for literally 1000 years.* This belief in *Chiliasm* or *millenarianism* was condemned due to its overly literal interpretation of the 20th chapter of Book of Revelation.

The next heresy to sprout promoted a false millenaristic doctrine which the Church summarized with the following adjectives*: false, earthly, crass, secular, radical, and carnal millenarianism.* Bearing synonymous titles, they all share the heretical doctrines of the establishment of an earthly kingdom imbibed with *carnal pleasures* of all sorts lasting for *literally* 1000 years. Christ, they say, will reign *physically and visibly* amidst his saints during this period of licentious and immoderate pleasures. One such proponent of this doctrine was the Gnostic Cerinthus whose writings flourished toward the end of the first century. It is noteworthy that although Augustine does not dismiss the possibility of a period of peace or "rest", he nonetheless concurs in condemning the notion of *carnal* millenarianism. Again, this heresy, known by various titles, had been condemned on account of its hedonistic interpretation of the same chapter of Revelation.

Next there arose "the millenarian doctrines of Montanus". About 170 A.D., Montanus founded the heretical sect known as the *montanists*, which based its belief on the conviction that the millenary kingdom had already begun and that the heavenly Jerusalem had descended upon the Phrygian borough of Pepuza (Asia Minor). This heresy was not officially rejected until centuries later. With the passing of time, the Church's collective anathemas against proponents of millenarianism eventually came to a standstill, as they had taken quite a toll on heresies which had already been successfully eradicated.

In the 16th century, Protestantism ushered in a new epoch of millenaristic doctrines. This heretical nuance promoted the belief in a new golden age under Christ, wherein the Papacy would be overthrown along with its secular empires. In 1534, this Protestant movement, known as the *Anabaptists,* set up the "new kingdom of Zion" as a prelude to the new kingdom to come. However, not even the Lutherans would support the Anabaptists in their quest for heaven's gate.

With the dawn of the 17th and 18th centuries, new apocalyptic heresies emerged. In certain countries, such as Germany, France and England, "Pietism" became increasingly fashionable in Protestant circles. Pietism was begun in the late

17th century by Jacob Spener who sought to awaken dormant Protestantism through an increased and intensified prayer life. From this focus on intense prayer, the name *Pietism* was derived. But in time this movement would also degenerate into strange forms of apocalyptic beliefs known as the ancient heresy of *Chiliasm* or *millenarianism*. Eva Buttlar preached a *spiritual millenaristic* doctrine, which, in turn, gave rise to the old hedonistic heresy known as *carnal millenarianism* of the *Labadists*. The roots of other heresies derived from these, with their antidogmatic and antihierarchical doctrines, could be found in the condemned heresies of the first few centuries. The sect of Pietism could be credited with their reemergence.

Shortly afterward, these pietistic doctrines were instituted within Catholic circles. The rebirth of the old heresy known as Chiliasm, would now be addressed under the new titles of *mitigated, modified or spiritual millenarianism*. This heresy is easily recognized by characteristics similar to those of its predecessors, with the one exclusion of carnal pleasures (hence the title "mitigated", "modified" or "spiritual"). In other words, as once held by the Chiliasts, the Pietists believed that before the General Judgment Christ would descend to earth *in the flesh* and reign visibly for *1000 years* ; however, he would not participate in immoderate carnal banquets.

It is noteworthy that the "spiritual blessings" of which Tertullian speaks — as, for example, when he says, "We say that this city has been provided by God for receiving the saints on their resurrection, and *refreshing them* with the abundance of all really spiritual blessings" (Adversus Marcion, *Ibid.*) — are never intended to convey the physical reign of Christ for literally 1000 years often associated with *spiritual millenarianism*. On the contrary, as can be theologically deduced from the biblical exegesis of the Fathers, these "spiritual blessings" refer to the blessings procured by God which cause the earth's rejoicing, i.e., "Let the heavens rejoice and earth be glad, let the *sea* and all within it *thunder* praise, let the *land and all it bears rejoice,* all the *trees* of the wood *shout* for joy, at the presence of the Lord for he comes, he comes to rule the earth" (cf. Ps. 96:13); "...For it is the seedtime of peace: the vine shall yield its fruit, the land shall bear its crops, and the heavens shall give their dew" (Zec. 8:12); "The earth shall yield its fruit, for God, our God has blessed us" (cf. Ps. 66:7).

Whereas the *spiritual millenarianists* retain the heresy of Christ's reign in the flesh for 1000 years, the Fathers concur in the doctrine of Christ's reign neither in the flesh nor for literally 1000 years, but from above and for a period of time simultaneous with the earth's rejoicing. Furthermore, they leave absolutely no room for the intervention of hedonistic or carnal indulgences. St. Thomas categorically testifies to this fact in presenting what was the traditional and orthodox view on the characteristics that pertain to God's rest with his saints: "The quoted text [Jer. 31:38] refers not to the carnal but to the *spiritual* Israel" (*Quaestiones Disputatae*, Vol. II *De Potentia*, Q. 5, Art. 5, Editrice Marietti, Roma, Italy, 1965, p. 140). Thus the "spiritual", when understood in light of the doctrines of the Church Fathers, in no way resembles those characteristics that derive from the heresy of "spiritual millenarianism".

Consequently, the Church officially condemned the theory *of mitigated, modified or spiritual millenarianism* in a formal declaration issued from the Holy See, thereby stifling once and for all any potential heretical resurgings of the past: *"Systema Millenarismi mitigati tuto doceri non posse"* [The system of mitigated Millenarianism cannot be safely taught] (*AAS, Ibid.*). This second condemnation in 1944 was necessary, as this heresy contradicted the revealed Catholic doctrine that Christ cannot come again *in the Father's glory, in the flesh and in human history* in order to establish an earthly kingdom before the Final Judgment (cf. *La Somma Teologica, IV Sent.*, Thomas Aquinas, edizione Studio Domenicano, Bologna, 1985, d.43,q.1,a.3,qc.1; *De Romano Pontefice*, Robert Bellarmine, 1.3, cap. 17, Neapoli, apud Josephum Giuliano, 1856 [cf. *Enciclopedia Cattolica*, Città del Vaticano, Ente per l'Enciclopedia Cattolica e per il libro Cattolico, 1948, p. 1010];

Mt. 16:27: *"Filius hominis venturus est in gloria Patris sui cum Angelis, tunc reddet unicuique secundum opera sua"* [For the Son of man will come with his Angels in his Father's glory, and then he will repay everyone according to his conduct]).

However, due to poor hermeneutical scholarship, several authors, following Eusebius' lead, began to attribute the anathematized doctrines of *mitigated millenarianism* to the orthodox doctrines of the Apostolic Fathers. Failing to incorporate the exegetical norms in the interpretation of the Fathers' ancient writings, the Apostolic Tradition on the millennium began to lose credibility, and the orthodoxy they vehemently professed to maintain was now in question. If we briefly examine the threefold objective of hermeneutics, this departure from Tradition on the part of certain modern-day scholars will become more evident.

The first objective is called *noematics* (from Greek *nòema):* to determine the nature of the different species of the biblical sense (i.e., of the truth which God, the principal author of the Bible, intends to express through the words written by the hagiographer, who is only the instrumental, or secondary author of the script); **the second** is called *heuristics* (from Greek eurìsko): to establish the interpretation of the Bible; and finally **the third** is *prophorisitics* (from Greek propsèro): to find the most convenient way of proposing, according to the various aptitudes of the readers, the true sense of the texts (cf. *Catholic Dictionary of Dogmatic Theology, Ibid.,* pp. 124-125). Given this, it follows that the intended *spiritual sense* employed by the Church Fathers was neither determined (noematics) nor established (heuristics) for the readers' understanding (prophoristics).

The Church's condemnations, therefore, are directed not toward the Fathers but toward all forms of chiliastic or millenaristic doctrines that fall under the collective umbrella of what is known today as *"a false millennium"* or more simply *"millenarianism"*. This all too literal interpretation of a millenary kingdom of God is the basis from which all suspicions of the early Fathers' professed orthodoxy are derived. The *Catholic Encyclopedia* reaffirms this in stating that "millenarianism is that thought which stems from a too literal, incorrect, and faulty interpretation of Chapter 20 of the Book of Revelation... This can only be understood in a *spiritual sense...*" (*Catholic Encyclopedia Revised,* Thomas Nelson, Nashville, TN, 1987, p. 387) which, as we have seen, is the "sense" employed by the Apostolic Fathers.

Furthermore, if we consider the pre-Vatican II era, in which many ecclesiastically approved books detailed the Church's doctrines as pronounced by her Magisterium, we discover the concept of a "millennium", an "age to come", an "era" of peace or "some mighty triumph of Christianity before the end" treated at length and accepted as sound doctrine.

For example, *The Teachings of the Catholic Church*, which bears the Church's required seals and was published in 1952 by a theological commission of qualified experts, clearly states that it is not contrary to Catholic teaching to believe or profess "a hope in some mighty triumph of Christ here on earth before the final consummation of all things. **Such an occurrence is not excluded, is not impossible,** it is not all certain that there will not be a prolonged period of triumphant Christianity before the end." The commission goes on to clarify the matter...

> *The point of division* between the legitimate aspirations of such devout believers and... *false* millenarism is this: the Chiliasts — as believers in the millennium are called, from the Greek word for a thousand — seem to expect a coming of Christ and a presence of him in glory and majesty *on this earth* which would not be the consummation of all things but would still be *a portion of the history of mankind.* This is not consonant Catholic dogma... The coming of

Christ in the second Advent... is the consummation of all things, the end of human history. *If before that final end there is to be a period, more or less prolonged, of triumphant sanctity, such a result will be brought about, not by the apparition of the Person of Christ in Majesty but by the operation of those powers of sanctification which are now at work, the Holy Ghost and the Sacraments of the Church.* The Chiliasts of all times... and there are many to be found even to date, seem to despair, not only of the world, but even of that dispensation of grace which was inaugurated at Pentecost; they expect from the *visible presence* of Christ a complete conversion of the world, as if such a happy result could not be otherwise brought about (*The Teaching of the Catholic Church: A Summary of Catholic Doctrine, Ibid.*).

The Church is stating here that only through works of sanctification — namely, those actions the Holy Church Councils have "appropriated" to the Third Person of the Blessed Trinity, the Holy Spirit — will such a "more or less prolonged period of triumphant sanctity" occur. Thus, the work of sanctification is not particular to the Second Person of the Trinity nor to the First; neither the Father nor the Son can bring about this period of sanctity, but rather, according to Tradition, it is the Holy Spirit's function to purify, transform, renew and *sanctify!*

In his commentary on Rom. 8:19-20, J.A. Fitzmyer states that the world will be "transformed by his Spirit" (*Jerome Biblical Commentary*, J.A. Fitzmyer, Prentice-Hall, Engelwood Cliffs, NJ, 1968). This serves as just one more reason to support the Church's traditional prayer, her *lex orandi* which has always invoked the Holy Spirit as the Sanctifier of the earth in order to restore it to its original pristine state: "Come, Holy Spirit fill the hearts of Thy faithful and kindle within them the fire of Thy

Love. Send forth Thy Spirit that we may be recreated and *Thou shalt renew the face of the earth.*"

In the early Church liturgy, in particular during the third century, the Holy Spirit played an eminent role in her life of worship. He was often invoked as the one who cleanses and sanctifies, as the one who prepares us for the Father. This is evidenced in the Lord's prayer which became "the centre of daily and liturgical prayer. It was solemnly entrusted (*traditio*) to the catechumen as the expression of his new birth" (*Encyclopedia of the Early Church,* Vol. II, Edited by Angelo DiBerardino, James Clarke & Co., Cambridge, England, 1992, p. 707). And it is precisely here, in the Lord's prayer (the "Our Father"), where we find that some early Church Fathers, such as Gregory of Nyssa, used the words, "May your Holy Spirit come upon us and cleanse us", as a substitue for the petition, "Your Kingdom come", thereby testifying to the truthfulness of the Tradition handed on by Papias, Irenaeus and Justin Martyr (see footnote to Luke 11:2 in the *New American Bible,* St. Joseph Edition, *Ibid.,* p. 119). These Fathers knew that the kingdom to come upon the earth must be the fruit of the Holy Spirit's sanctifying action.

Through the Holy Spirit, the Sanctifier, Christ is able to bring salvation history to fulfillment. The Church tells us that if "before that final end there is to be a period, more or less prolonged of triumphant sanctity, such a result will be wrought not by the apparition of the Person of Christ in Majesty but by... the Holy Spirit"; in doing so, she attests to those powers of sanctification that are appropriated to the Holy Spirit. It is no wonder, then, that our reigning Pontiff in his recent Apostolic Letter stated, "During this important time... unity among all Christians of the various confessions will increase until they reach full communion... We are all aware, however, that the attainment of this goal cannot be the fruit of human efforts alone, vital as they are. Unity, after all, is a gift of the Holy Spirit" (*Tertio Millennio Adveniente, Ibid.,* 16, 34). In other words, the Holy Spirit, the glorified Spirit of Christ, is glorified with the Father and the Son in the reflection of their Triune communion in all creation, by bringing about **"a period, more or less prolonged, of triumphant sanctity before that final end"**.

St. Bernard of Clairvaux (1090—1153)

St. Bernard, Abbot and Doctor, was a typical exponent of what many modern scholars call monastic theology, which "aims at a clear, orderly, warm exposition of the truth, such as will serve to dispose the soul to prayer and contemplation" (*New Catholic Encyclopedia, Ibid.*, Vol. III, p. 337). St. Bernard's theology, doctrinally sound, does not share those fanciful novelties that other theologies profess, but rather reiterates that which the Apostles handed down and which the Church upholds. The Church, in fact, states that his doctrines are "not distinguished by the discovery of new modes of thought or the achievement of new conclusions...Bernard's sources were principally the Scriptures, then the Fathers of the Church" (*Ibid.*).

And yet, it is precisely Bernard, ever faithful to Tradition, who waxes eloquent with the following exposition on the temporal kingdom:

> We know that **there are three comings of the Lord.** The third lies between the other two. It is *invisible,* while the other two are visible. In the first coming, He was seen on earth, dwelling among men; He Himself testifies that they saw Him and hated Him. In the final coming, "all flesh will see the salvation of our God, and they will look upon Him whom they pierced". **The intermediate coming is a hidden one; in it *only the elect* see the Lord within their own selves,** and they are saved. In his first coming,

our Lord came in our flesh and in our weakness; **in this middle coming, He is our rest and consolation.**

In case someone should think that this middle coming is sheer invention, listen to what our Lord Himself says: "If anyone loves me, he will keep my word, and my Father will love him, and we will come to him" (Sermo 5, *Adventu Domini, 1-3,* Bernard of Clairvaux, in *Opera Omnia,* Edit. Cisterc. 4 [1966] 188-190; reference taken from *The Liturgy of the Hours,* Catholic Book Pub. Co., NY, 1975, Vol. I, p. 169).

Bernard, like several of the early Fathers, strongly insists that no one dismiss this "middle coming" as the product of sheer human invention, but rather that they accept it together with the doctrines of the Apostolic Tradition, with which he was acutely familiar.

St. Thomas Aquinas (1225 — 1274) and St. Robert Bellarmine (1542 — 1621)

St. Thomas Aquinas, the only Doctor to have received the title *Doctor Angelicus* (great theological import) and *Doctor Communis* (universal and timelessness character of his teaching), is regarded by many as the greatest Doctor in Catholic Church history. In his monumental *Quaestiones Disputatae,* Thomas sustains the doctrine of a *"rest" beyond time,* while touching upon the concept of a terrestrial kingdom of God. This "rest" insofar as it alludes to God's definitively established kingdom, nonetheless attests to the common opinion in Tradition that in God's eternal Kingdom nothing can be measured according to our estimation of time, being itself beyond time. Aquinas' theology in this regard is a cardinal point in view of what we have already stated: that in God's Kingdom, there can be no "time". Whether temporary or eternal, both constitute one kingdom inasmuch as the former, possessing similar characteristics of the latter, is its integral prelude. Time will assume new meaning; it will not be the same as we know it. Because all creation will undergo a transformation in the kingdom to come, any attempt to now measure its duration according to our standards — the present orbital solar and lunar systems that separate days from nights — will prove impossible. Thomas explains this point in further detail:

> The heavenly movement will end in an instant: and in that instant there will be... the end of movement and the beginning of [eternal] rest. The subsequent rest **will not be in time**, because rest is measured by time not directly, but indirectly... Even as the celestial movement will cease, so also **will time be no more**, as appears from the text quoted from Apocalypse... At the beginning of the world nature was being established... at the end of the world the operation of nature will attain the end appointed by God (*Quaestiones Disputatae, Ibid.*).

And it is partly due to the fact that time cannot be directly measured that the Church has swiftly condemned the heresy of a temporary or millenary kingdom lasting for *literally 1000 years*. This cannot be possible based upon the laws of the nature of time which will undergo a transformation during this rest. Thomas further explains:

> As Augustine says, the last age of the world corresponds to the last stage of man's life, which **does not last for a fixed number of years** as the other stages do, but lasts sometimes as long as the others together, and even longer. Wherefore the last age of the world **cannot be assigned a fixed number of years or generations** (*Ibid.*).

The "millenary interspace" cannot occur in **our** estimation of time; nor can it be calculated by an exact number of years. Even if one were to adopt a literal interpretation of a thousand years of peace, it would be disproved by Lactantius' statement on the millennium of peace, as it falls shy of a thousand years: "**Before** the end of the thousand years, the devil shall be loosed afresh and shall assemble all the pagan nations to make war against the holy city."

This uncertain extension of years ascribed to the temporal kingdom thus seconds that period wherein **our** estimation of time is not ascribable. However, time, in the sense of its being regulated by sun and moon, will cease altogether only in the very end, that is, at the end of human history and the General Judgment of all the dead.

Since time is currently characterized by the regulation of days and nights, time in the temporal kingdom will be different from our current ways of estimation. On the other hand, time in the definitive kingdom, the New Jerusalem, will receive the reward of its labors and cease altogether. Still, because the temporary kingdom will have a sevenfold increase of light activity during the millennium, it follows that some sort of radical transformation in the arrangement of time will occur. The vehemence of the sun and moon's increased activity will of itself abolish all darkness, as is attested to in the following:

> The light of the moon will be like that of the sun and the light of the sun will be seven times greater (like the light of seven days) (Is. 30:26).

> I will turn darkness into light before them (Is. 42:16).

> Then the righteous will shine like the sun in the kingdom of their Father. Whoever has ears ought to hear (Mt. 13:43).

With the moon inheriting the sun's intensity, time will

no longer follow our standards of day and night. Due to the supernatural, luminescent magnification of both the sun and moon, the parameters of our chronological arrangement of events will be unequivocally altered. However, this does not preclude the continuance of the movement of the heavenly bodies: "From one new moon to another, and from one Sabbath to another, all mankind shall come to worship before me, says the Lord" (Is. 66:23). It appears, therefore, that only after the temporal kingdom of light that there will take place what St. Thomas calls "the cessation of the movements of the heavenly bodies".

As we shall later address in our exposition of Sacred Scripture, the temporal kingdom is quite distinct from the definitive kingdom in which the sun and moon will neither set nor rise again. After the millennium, the earth will no longer depend upon these heavenly illuminaries to sustain it: "No more shall the sun be your light by day, nor the brightness of the moon shine upon you at night; the Lord shall be your light forever, your God shall be your glory. No longer shall your sun go down, or your moon withdraw, for the Lord will be your light forever" (cf. Is. 60:19, 20); "The city had no need of sun or moon to shine on it, for the glory of God gave it light, and its lamp was *the Lamb*" (Rv. 21:23-24). In short, the sun and moon will be eclipsed by the light of Christ who has become the Light of the world, the Sustainer of the New heavens and the New earth.

Since it appears that the end of the rising and setting of the sun and moon will occur after the millennium, we are not to interpret their increase of light as the end of salvation history, but only of a transformation of time as we know it.

According to Catholic Tradition, the "end of human history" signifies the end of three principal themes: a) God's providential action and the various phases of the divine plan in relation to the human race as contained in revelation; b) man's free response to the divine action; c) the struggle between the forces of good and evil, grace and sin, God and Satan. The Church considers St. Augustine's exposition on human history as being supreme. His vast yet simple concept describes "Two Loves" building two cities or two commonwealths, which exist side by side as invisible protagonists from the beginning to the end of history, "both locked in conflict and competition throughout the ages and providing the dynamic historical development until the issue shall be decided between them, in the grand denouncement of the Parousia, the Last Judgment, and the triumph of Christ and the Church" (*New Catholic Encyclopedia, Ibid.*, Vol. VII, p. 27).

When the millennium occurs, it will not be the end, but will be followed by "the Last Judgment" and definitive "triumph of Christ and the Church". At that point, man's pilgrim state will come to an end and history will cease. But man himself will not cease to be.

God's providential action in the Church will continue during the temporal kingdom, where Christ will reign in the Eucharist in relation to the human race, and mankind will continue to have free response to the divine action. The saints who possess this kingdom, Scriptures and Church Fathers testify, will continue to work and sleep, to plant and eat, to procreate and build up God's earthly city of love. From this we perceive the need for the continuance of both the sun and the moon...

> For as the days of the tree of life, so shall be the days of My people, and the works of their hands shall be multiplied. My elect shall not labor in vain, nor bring forth children for a curse; for they shall be a righteous seed blessed by the Lord, and their posterity with them. And it shall come to pass that before they call, I will hear... Then the wolves and lambs shall feed together, and the lion shall eat like the ox, and the serpent shall eat earth like bread. They shall not hurt nor

destroy on my holy mountain, saith the Lord...
(Is. 65:17-25 in Dialogue with Trypho, *Ibid.*).

Thus, the temporal kingdom will be an extraordinary event in human history, where man will toil under the sun, but not in vain (Is. 65:23). It will be an expression of God's bounty toward humankind and a prelude to the definitive kingdom to come. The doctrine of Christ's return in the flesh and the end of history is further developed in the following ecclesiastical statements when speaking of the necessity of Christ's return to this earth in glory and majesty in order to complete salvation history:

> The Last Judgment will come when Christ returns in glory. Only the Father knows the day and the hour; only he determines the moment of its coming. Then through his Son Jesus Christ he will pronounce **the final word on all history**... The Last Judgment will reveal that God's justice triumphs over all the injustices committed by his creatures and that God's love is stronger than death (*CCC, Ibid.*, 1040);

and:

> *False* millenarianism is this: the Chiliasts — as believers in the millennium are called, from the Greek word for a thousand — seem to expect a coming of Christ and a presence of him in glory and majesty **on this earth** which would not be the consummation of all things but would still be **a portion of the history of mankind**. This is not consonant Catholic dogma... *(The Teaching of the Catholic Church: A Summary of Catholic Doctrine, Ibid.).*

And this provides us with the response to a rebuttal made by an author who stated, "The entire Catholic Tradition on this subject [the millennium] from the time of the Fathers till now consistently teaches that the Parousia comes a reasonably **short time** after the death of Antichrist." He then attempts to prove this by quoting St. Robert Bellarmine, "For Antichrist shall come a *short time* before the end of the world."

What the author fails to consider is the twofold interpretation the Fathers have given to Antichrist. While "the ancient Fathers identify the Beast with Antichrist" [who is thrown into the fiery lake *before* the millennium Rv. 19:20-21] (*The Book of Destiny,* Rev. H.B. Kramer, TAN Books and Publishers, Inc., Rockford, IL, 1975, p. 260), they also convey a reprisal of the spirit of Antichrist through Gog, chief prince of Magog, when the 1000 years are almost completed (The Divine Institutes, *Ibid.*).

It is also interesting how St. Thomas Aquinas clarifies this author's misconception of time without contradicting St. Bellarmine in the least. Thomas states, "These words of Scripture that would seem to indicate **shortness of time or nearness of the end, are not so much to be referred to the amount of time** as to a certain disposition of the present state of the world" (*Quaestiones Disputatae, Ibid.*). Time to which one cannot attach a certain number of days is not to be measured directly nor according to our estimation of eventual succession. The words of the inspired writers of Sacred Scripture and the Apostolic Tradition clarify time in this regard: "Do not be ignorant of this one fact, beloved, that with the Lord one day is like a thousand years and a thousand years like one day" (cf. 2 Pt. 3:8); "To your eyes a thousand years are like yesterday, come and gone, no more than a watch in the night" (cf. Ps. 90:4); "Now... we understand that **a period of one thousand years is indicated in symbolic language**" (Dialogue with Trypho, *Ibid.*); etc. Whence proceeds the Holy See's pronouncement that Christ cannot come again **in the flesh, in human history** in order to establish an earthly kingdom **lasting exactly 1000 years** before the Final Judgment: *"systema Millenarismi mitigati tuto doceri non posse"* ["The system of mitigated Millenarianism cannot be safely taught"] (*Acta*

Apostolicae Sedis, Ibid.). This, as we have seen, is based particularly upon the doctrines of St. Thomas Aquinas and St. Robert Bellarmine: *De Romano Pontefice*, 1.3, cap. 17; Mt. 16:27: *"Filius hominis venturus est **in gloria Patris sui** cum Angelis, tunc reddet unicuique secundum opera sua"* ["For the Son of man will come with his Angels **in his Father's glory**, and then he will repay everyone according to his conduct"].

The doctrines of Holy Mother Church, embellished by those of Tertullian, Augustine, Bernard, Aquinas, Bellarmine and others, are clear: a temporary terrestrial kingdom of God before the end of the world can only take place beyond our current understanding of time. Thus, it is safe to conclude that one cannot arrive at an absolute estimate of its duration.

Based upon the doctrines of these holy Doctors and the combined sources of Scripture and Tradition, the Catholic Catechism has developed the following teachings on the future kingdom of Christ. Exercising the Church's ordinary Magisterium, it unequivocally places Christ's triumphant and definitive reign outside of human history:

> The Antichrist's deception already begins to take shape in the world every time the claim is made to realize within history **that messianic hope which can only be realized beyond history** through the eschatological judgment (*CCC, Ibid.*, 676).

> The kingdom will be fulfilled, then, **not by a historic triumph** of the Church through a progressive ascendancy, but only by God's victory over the final unleashing of evil, which will cause the bride to come down from heaven (*CCC, Ibid.*, 677).

> The Last Judgment will come when Christ returns in glory. Only the Father knows the day and the hour; only he determines the moment of

its coming. Then through his Son Jesus Christ he will pronounce **the final word on all history** ... The Last Judgment will reveal that God's justice triumphs over all the injustices committed by his creatures and that God's love is stronger than death (*CCC, Ibid.*, 1040).

CHAPTER 4

SACRED SCRIPTURE SPEAKS

The teaching of the apostles, known to us today as the *Apostolic Tradition,* began with their preaching (kèrygma). Indeed, the apostles preached Christ according to Scripture: Christ was the fulfillment of Scripture and the focal point from which they derived their significance. By demonstrating how the historical Christ was the response to Old Testament prophecies, the apostles' preaching and Tradition revealed the entire structure of the economy of salvation, whose center was Christ. Their doctrinal Tradition, therefore, consisted in a method of Scriptural presentation which, as we have seen, became the method of presentation of the Apostolic Fathers. Like the Apostles, the Fathers were unanimous in asserting that the true understanding of Scripture is only found in the Church, and it is from this that there arose Tradition. This longstanding theological development aiding in the understanding of Scriptures, embodied and represented by the understanding of the Apostles and Fathers is, therefore, constituent of this teaching called the Apostolic Tradition.

It is significant that, while Tradition may be closely linked to Scripture, Tradition is not Scripture. Scripture is an inspired series of canonical books whose contents, when interpreted in the light of the Apostles, the Fathers and the Magisterium, become pedagogic and salvific. Tradition, on the other hand, while expressing a continuity with Scripture, exceeds the parameters of that which had been grasped and understood as the revealed Word of God. For as revelation progresses, the Church teaches us, it includes the totality of the truth under the guidance and influence of the Holy Spirit.

Thus, Tradition transmits the pure and simple revelation of God's Word in Sacred Scripture; in addition, however, it further explains this Word. In this respect, Scripture is explained by Apostolic Tradition, without the latter ever departing from its point of origin, the deposit of faith. Wherefore when speaking of the doctrines of the Apostolic Fathers and of those distinguished Doctors who have expounded upon their scholarship, we cannot overlook the fact that their efforts in penetrating the Sacred texts have been so successful that the truth is now more accessible to us than during the time of the Apostles. To reject what one does not find formally in Sacred Scripture is to disavow oneself from the Catholic teaching of "the development of doctrine".

Consequently, it would indeed seem imprudent for anyone to reject the Fathers' doctrines on the temporal kingdom. With utmost fidelity to apostolic teachings, the Fathers bear witness to this unbroken and homogenous progression, the Apostolic Tradition. Incorporated within it, furthermore, are the doctrines on the General Judgment.

These doctrines, in particular, range from the universal punishment of all evildoers to the resurrection and judgment of all the dead. Although they may initially seem peripheral, these doctrines are of cardinal importance, as they disclose the Fathers' theology on the millennium. If we are to grasp their theological import, a serious assessment of the General Judgment is in order. Therefore, included below is a comparative listing of the doctrines on the General Judgment as contained in the biblical exegesis of the Fathers. Let us begin with the text of St. Peter the Apostle, including at this juncture the divisions of the Fathers [in brackets]...

The heavens existed of old and earth was formed out of water *[creation]*... the world that then existed was destroyed, deluged with water" *[end of 1st heavens & earth: the remnant of Noah's family]*. The present heavens and earth have been reserved by the same word for fire, kept for the day of destruction of the godless *[1st instance of judgment]*. But...one day is like *a thousand years* and a thousand years like one day... the Day of the Lord will come like a thief *[2nd heavens & earth: the remnant of the millennium]*, and *then* the heavens will pass away with a mighty roar and the elements will be dissolved by fire, and the earth and everything done on it will be found out *[2nd instance of judgment]*... But according to his promise we await new heavens and a new earth" *[3rd heavens & earth: the final remnant of the New Jerusalem or eternal paradise]* (2 Pt. 3:5-13).

The second heavens and earth are distinct from the third heavens and earth, insofar as the former possess those characteristics peculiar to a limited duration, whereas the latter to a nature that is endless. While the second and third heavens and earth have been distinguished by the respective adjectives "transformed" and "New", they may both be called "new", inasmuch as they both exceed our current laws governing time; they subsist within a "new" dimension. Wherefore in those approved private revelations by God or the Blessed Mother, where they have been reported to have stated that humanity is on the threshold of "new" heavens and "new" earth, this is to be understood not as the end of human history (the New Jerusalem), but as the inception of the millennium: the temporary kingdom of God and his saints.

The reason for the divisions of two instances of the General Judgment is not to indicate two separate Judgments or comings, but rather a blending of these two instances. The Church teaches us that when Christ returns for the second time, he will judge both the living and the dead. This event is known as *The Day of the Lord*. It will contain a judgment of the *living* and a judgment of the *dead*. The *first instance* will inaugurate the reign of God's Will and the transformation of time as the preparatory phase for the end of the *second instance*, which concludes all time and human history. The two instances constitute one judgment insofar as they are applied as one event to this whole complex of the divine operation, that is the General Judgment of the *living* and that of the *dead* as a blending of these two ideas or instances. Tradition holds that there will be one General Judgment, comprised of two events (the judgment of the living **and** that of the dead; *"venturus est judicare vivos et mortuos"*). This is further exemplified in the scriptural texts of Rv. 19:14: first instance: Christ descends to sanctify the earth by means of his glorified Spirit, accompanied by his heavenly hosts; and Rv. 20:11: second instance: Christ is seated on the throne.

Earlier, we touched upon the two instances in the writings of Lactantius. In keeping with the Fathers' theology and that of their succeeding Ecclesiastical Writers, we see, through the presentation of those blended characteristics that pertain to the first and second instance, the biblical foundation of which they availed themselves to explain and develop the traditional doctrines of the Apostles.

1. First Instance of Christ's General Judgment

The following characteristics are peculiar to the first instance:

Jesus *descends from the heavens* **by way of his purifying Spirit,** *the armies follow him, judgment comes by the sword* **and** *of the living* **only and it occurs** *suddenly,* **in** *"an hour"* **or** *"a Day"* ("Day" not to be taken literally, but indicating a period of time). These traits are evidenced in texts such as:

a. Judgment Comes Through Jesus and by Way of the Sword

"When my *sword* has drunk its fill in the heavens, lo, it shall come down in judgment..." (Is. 34:5).

"To all who inhabit the earth to its very ends the uproar spreads; for the Lord [Jesus] has an indictment against the nations, he is to *pass judgment* upon all mankind: The godless shall be given to *the sword*, says the Lord... A great storm is unleashed from the ends of the earth" (Jer. 25:31, 32).

"...all the nations shall see *the judgment* I have executed... All of them [all the living] fell by *the sword*... (Ez. 39:21).

"...*a sharp two-edged sword came out of his mouth*, and his face shone like the sun in its brightness" (Rv. 1:16).

"The rest were killed by *the sword* that came out of the mouth of the one riding on the horse..." (Rv. 19:21).

"Then I saw the heavens opened, and there was a white horse; its rider was called 'Faithful and True.' *He judges* and wages war in righteousness...*The armies of heaven followed him,* mounted on white horses and wearing clean white linen. Out of his mouth came *a sharp sword* to strike the nations" (Rv. 19:11-15).

N.B. "The *armies of heaven followed him*...wearing clean white linen" (Rv. 19:14). Rv. 7:9, 13; 19:8; and 14:13 conjointly tell us that "the white linen represents the righteous deeds of the holy ones, whereas Rv. 15:6 says that the *seven Angels* are adorned in white linen. When one speaks, therefore, of the *armies of heaven following him*, whether they are "mounted on white horses and wearing clean white linen, coming down with Christ to pronounce judgment," or simply "holy ones" of whom white is a symbol of righteous deeds, one may safely say that the armies are intended as both those *seven Angels* to whom are given the censors of God's wrath to execute justice upon all the nations, as well as the just and "holy ones".

The often-invoked expressions, "the coming of Christ", or "the return of Christ", although allusive of his final coming in the flesh, are also used in several Church-approved private revelations to indicate a *spiritual* descent of Christ referred to by St. Bernard as "the intermediate coming of Christ". While the Son, on the one hand, is traditionally regarded as the Protagonist at the end of human history ("he will come again to judge the living and the dead"), it is the Holy Spirit who prepares the world to receive him again through the infusion of his operative gifts in the souls of the faithful.

While acknowledging their consubstantiality, but so as to avoid confusing their operations, Holy Mother Church, in her Councils, has attributed certain characteristics that pertain to each of the divine Persons: "To the **Father** are attributed the operations of power, creation, omnipotence, the sending of his Son into the world, etc.; to the **Son** are attributed the operations of wisdom, reconciliation of man with God, the revelation of the mystery of the Trinity to the world, the mediator of creation and *salvation,* redemption, etc.; to the **Spirit** are attributed the operations of love, divine bounty, the Incarnation of the Word, the conception and birth of Jesus Christ (the sending forth of Christ), sanctification of souls, inhabitation, assistance in creation and *salvation history,* etc." (*Enchiridion Symbolorum, Ibid.*). The Father creates, the Son redeems and the Spirit sanctifies. The mystical doctor, St. John of the Cross, in keeping with Tradition, states that such sanctification cannot be wrought save by way of the Spirit's preceding operations of purgation, illumination and unification. And although he is placed after the Father and the Son, it is not a consequence of *subordination,* but of his final role in the economy of salvation history.

94

Conversely, it is also a dogma of faith that the Three Divine Persons are inseparable. When one Person operates, the other Two are in some manner present and active in that operation: *"...Nec tamen tres personae separabilis aestimandae sunt, cum nulla ants aliam nulla post aliam, nulla sine alia vel exsitisse, vel quidpiam operasse aliquando credatur"* — "No one ought to esteem these three Persons as separable, for we believe that neither of these three Persons has existed or operated before, after or without any of the others" (*Enchiridion Symbolorum, Ibid.*).

The Son, therefore, while unique and consubstantial with the Father and the Spirit, is regarded by the author of the Book of Revelation as the protagonist of the end times who receives assistance from the other two divine Persons. And it is here where the spiritual descent of Christ comes into play. Because Christ will not descend in the flesh in human history, he will come by way of his glorified Spirit who will purge, illuminate and unify all creation. This is just one example where both the Son and the Spirit are present and active in the same operation. Intimately united with the Father, both the Son and Spirit, in virtue of their consubstantial and collaborative effort in salvation history, will bring about the transformation and unification of creation. This process, referred to as Christ's spiritual descent through his Spirit, is evidenced by Gregory of Nyssa and other early Church Fathers' usage of the words, "May your Holy Spirit come upon us and cleanse us", as a substitution for the petition, "Your Kingdom come" in the Lord's prayer (*New American Bible*, St. Joseph's Edition, *Ibid.*, p. 119).

b. Judgment Is Passed Upon Those That Are Alive, Not Those Who Have Already Received Their Particular Sentence, Not the Dead

"...to announce to those *who dwell on earth*... His time

has come" (Rv. 14:6, 7).

Judgment on the evildoers: "You are just, O Holy One, who are and who were, in passing this sentence. For they have shed the blood of the holy ones and the prophets..." (Rv. 16:5, 6).

"...judgment on the great harlot who *lives*..." (Rv. 17:1).

"...God has judged..."; "...He has *condemned*..." (Rv. 18:20;19.2).

"...he judges and wages war... the beast was caught and with it the false prophet... The two were thrown *alive* into the fiery pool..." (Rv. 19:11, 20).

The rest of the *evildoers are judged*: "The rest were killed by the sword that came out of the mouth of the one riding the horse, and all the birds gorged themselves on their flesh" (Rv. 19:21).

c. Judgment Is Carried Out Suddenly, Unlike the Second Instance Where Judgment Is Preceded by Signs

"Terrible and swiftly shall he come against you, because judgment is stern for the exalted..." (Wis. 6:5).

"And suddenly there will come to the temple the Lord whom you seek... But who can endure the day of his coming?" (Mal. 3:1-2).

"I will draw near to you for judgment, and I will be swift to bear witness" (Mal. 3:5).

"Suddenly there shall come upon you ruin which you will not expect" (Is. 47:11).

"When people are saying, 'Peace and security,' then

sudden disaster comes upon them, like labor pains upon a pregnant woman..." (1 Thes. 5:3-4).

"But the *Day of the Lord* will come *like a thief...*" (2 Pt. 3:10; the succeeding verse shifts, as do those of other passages, to the second instance, thereby homogenizing the two events into one General Judgment: "*and then* the heavens will pass away with a mighty roar and the elements will be dissolved by fire...").

"Behold, I am coming like a thief" (Rv. 16:15).

N.B. "The coming of the Son of man" in Scripture and Tradition has been applied to both instances of the General Judgment. This is not to imply that there are three visible comings of Christ, but rather two divine interventions of Christ after the Incarnation. The first will be by way of his Spirit who will come to purify and sanctify the earth of all iniquity. This will be occasioned by *the apparition* of the Person of Christ in the heavens who will come in his glorified Spirit. However, in this first instance, Christ does not remain on the earth to dwell in the flesh with his saints. This will be realized in the second, when he descends in the flesh in his own Person, and not simply by way of his glorified Spirit, for the second and final time to definitively restore all things in himself and thus give glory to his Father.

d. Judgment Comes in an *Hour* or in a *Day*

"For the Lord has *a Day* of vengeance..." (Is. 34:8).

"...I will take away the guilt of the land *in one Day*" (Zec. 3:9).

"For you yourselves know very well that *the Day of the Lord* will come upon you like a thief at night" (1 Thes. 5:2).

"*In one hour* this great wealth has been ruined" (Rv. 18:17).

"...alas, great city...*in one hour* she has been ruined" (Rv. 18:19).

"*In one hour* your judgment has come" (Rv. 18:10).

The First Instance of Judgment in Ezekiel and the Book of Revelation

"Thus I will display my glory among the nations, and all the nations shall see *the judgment* I have executed and the hand I have laid upon them. From that day forward the house of Israel shall know that I am the Lord, their God... All of them *[the living]* fell by *the sword*... *Now I will restore* the fortunes of Jacob and have pity on the whole house of Israel... I will bring them back from among the peoples, *I will gather them* from the lands of their enemies, and will prove My holiness through them in the sight of all the nations" (cf. Ez. 39:21-27).

"He *judges* and wages war in righteousness... Out of his mouth came a sharp sword to strike the nations...The beast was caught and with it the false prophet... The two were thrown alive into the fiery pool burning with sulfur. The rest were killed by the sword that came out of the mouth of the one riding on the horse..."(Rv. 19:11, 15, 20-21).

N.B. This judgment of "the one riding on the horse" clearly precedes the establishment of the temporary kingdom, designated a few verses later as "the camp of the holy ones and the beloved city" (Rv. 20:9). *After* this judgment "by the sword" (Rv. 19:11-21: first instance), and the establishment of the beloved city (Rv. 20:9), will occur the judgment "by fire" (Rv. 20:9-15, second instance): "But fire came down from heaven... The Devil... was thrown into the pool of fire and sulfur, where the beast and the false prophet were. There they will be tormented day and night forever and ever... *The dead were judged according to their deeds...* Anyone whose name was not found written in the book of life was thrown into the pool of fire" (Rv. 20:9-15).

The First Instance of Judgment in the Pauline Epistles

"We ask you, brothers, with regard to the coming of our Lord Jesus Christ and *our assembling with him*, not to be shaken out of your minds suddenly... that the day of the Lord is at hand. Let no one deceive you in any way. For unless *the apostasy comes first* and the lawless one is revealed, the one doomed to perdition... whom the Lord [Jesus] *will kill with the breath of his mouth* and render powerless by the manifestation of his coming... *that all who have not believed the truth* but have approved wrongdoing *may be condemned...* God chose you as the first fruits..." (2 Thes. 2:1-13).

"For we believe that Jesus died and rose, so too will God, through Jesus, *bring with him those who have fallen asleep.* Indeed, we tell you this, on the word of the Lord, that we *who are alive, who are left until the coming of the Lord*, will surely not precede *those who have fallen asleep.* For the Lord himself, with a word of command, with the voice of an Archangel and with the trumpet of God, will come down from heaven, and the *dead in Christ will rise first.* Then we *who are alive, who are left*, will be caught up together with them in the clouds to meet the Lord in the clouds. Thus we shall always be with the Lord" (1 Thes. 4:14-18).

If we carefully analyze these Pauline texts, we begin to uncover a sequence of eschatological events. It is clear that Paul places *"we who are alive, who are left until the coming of the Lord"* before "the Lord's coming". But is this "coming" of Christ his first or second instance of judgment?

The answer is disclosed in the next sentence: *"For the*

99

*Lord himself, with the voice of an Archangel and **with the trumpet** of God, will come down from heaven"*. The trumpet of God, therefore, ushers in our Lord's return. And where do we hear of such a trumpet inaugurating our Lord's triumphant return if not in the Book of Revelation: *"The **seventh angel blew his trumpet**. There were loud voices in heaven, saying, 'The kingdom of the world now belongs to our Lord and to his Anointed, and he will reign **forever and ever**.' The twenty-four elders who sat on their thrones before God...said: 'We give thanks to you, Lord God almighty... For you... have **established** your reign... Your wrath has come, and **the time to judge the dead**..."* (Rv. 11:15-19). The characteristics [in bold italics] which Paul describes are none other then those of the second instance of the General Judgment (cf. Joel 2:1-2, "Blow the *trumpet* in Zion...their like has not been seen from of old, *nor will it be after them"*). In the second instance, Christ judges *"the dead"*; his kingdom is definitively *"established"*, *"forever and ever"*, and not for a "period" or an "era", but for eternity.

In the same breath Paul adds, *"And the **dead** in Christ will rise first,"* thereby signifying the resurrection of the bodies of those who have already died in Christ, appropriated to the second instance of the General Judgment. He continues: *"Then we who are **alive**, who are left, will be caught up together with them in the clouds."* The words "we who are alive, and left" can only indicate one thing: a group of individuals who have been "left", who have remained on earth during a certain period of time.

And who could these individuals possibly be? St. Paul's second letter clarifies the matter: *"With regard to the coming of our Lord Jesus Christ and **our assembling with him**, not to be shaken out of your minds suddenly... that the day of the Lord is at hand. Let no one deceive you in any way. For **unless the apostasy comes first** and the lawless one is revealed, the one doomed to perdition... And then the lawless one will be revealed, whom the Lord Jesus will kill with the **breath of his mouth"*** (2 Thes. 2:1-8). Notice here that Paul, like the Church

Fathers, places the apostasy and the lawless one (Antichrist) before the first instance of the judgment of Christ. And as we have seen, to the first instance of judgment is appropriated the characteristic of Christ defeating Satan (through his minister, Antichrist) with his sword: *"Out of his mouth came a sharp sword to strike..."* (Rv. 19:15). This precedes the "assembling" with Christ, that is, the assembling of those *"who are alive, who are left,"* and who shall remain until the second instance in which Christ will judge *the dead.* It follows that "they" are those who have survived the first instance, having been found worthy to remain on earth, but on a transformed earth until the judgment of the dead.

They who are *left* on earth will be those who are found worthy to inherit the temporal kingdom which precedes the second instance of judgment. According to St. Paul, they wait to be *"caught up together with them [the dead in Christ who will rise first] in the clouds to meet the Lord. Thus we shall always be with the Lord".*

Lastly, the "first fruits" of which Paul speaks are none other than that remnant who have inherited the temporal kingdom and who anticipate the definitively established kingdom of God on earth, the New Jerusalem. They will have the privilege of foretasting a semblance of the New Jerusalem before it descends from heaven in *all* its beauty, "like a bride adorned for her husband" (Rv. 21:2). Accompanying this remnant into the New Jerusalem will be those generated during the millennium who survived Satan's last uprising (cf. the characteristic of procreation in Chapter 5), after the thousand years of his confinement, and those who have been liberated from purgatory, now abolished.

This remnant of the millennium, Lactantius eloquently states, will be comprised of all the just since the beginning of creation: *"But He, when He shall have destroyed unrighteousness, and executed His great judgment, and shall have recalled to life the righteous, who have lived from the beginning, will be engaged among men a thousand years"* (The Divine Institutes, *Ibid.*). Furthermore, the ordinary Magisterium of the Church declares that *"all the just who live during this time have a first resurrection..." (The Faith Explained, Ibid.,* p. 182). And Sacred Scripture attests to this in Psalm 149, which sings the new song reserved for the elect of the new earth:

> Sing to the Lord a new song, a hymn in the assembly of the faithful. Let Israel be glad in their maker, the people of Zion rejoice in their king... Let *the faithful* rejoice in their glory, cry out for joy at their banquet, with the praise of God in their mouths, and a two-edged sword in their hands, to bring retribution on the nations, punishment on the peoples, to bind their kings in chains and their nobles in fetters of iron, to execute judgment decreed for them — such is the glory of *all God's faithful.* Alleluia (passim Ps. 149).

Here we encounter praise of God with song and sword. This song of praise, further mentioned in the Book of Revelation, is heard coming from "a great multitude" who cry out "the wedding feast of the Lamb has begun!" Hence the "beginning" of the Lord's Day.

This hymn, furthermore, is said to be "a new hymn... No one could learn this hymn except the hundred and forty-four thousand who had been ransomed from the earth" (Rv. 14:3). It is also noteworthy that this hymn is sung "in the assembly of the faithful" at a time when judgment by the sword is being passed.

This "assembly of the faithful" strongly suggests the aforementioned assembly of which St. Paul spoke: "With regard to the coming of our Lord Jesus Christ and *our assembling with him...* Let no one deceive you in any way. For unless the apostasy comes first and the lawless one is revealed, the one doomed to perdition... And then the lawless one will be revealed, whom the Lord [Jesus] *will kill with the breath of his mouth* and render powerless by the manifestation of his coming..." (2 Thes. 2:1-9). Consequently, it appears that the song and sword of Psalm 149 are a prophecy of the first instance of judgment as prophesied in the Book of Revelation, where judgment is accompanied by an assembly, a song and a sword.

It is essential to emphasize the *first fruits* of that remnant which undergo a first resurrection. They will reign with Christ, but not in the sense of Christ gloriously reigning in his Person and in the flesh; Christ will not remain with them on earth save by way of the Eucharist. We shall address this in greater detail in our next chapter.

Regarding the first resurrection, it is peculiar to those who have died in Christ. The "dead" who will not rise until the thousand years are over (Rv. 20:5) refers not to those who have died *in Christ* and experienced a first resurrection, but to all the dead who have been either detained in purgatory or condemned to hell. These will come to life at the second instance of the General Judgment, reserved for the meting out of justice to those whose judgment was ratified but not consummated; now joined to their bodies, they will receive their definitive and eternal reward or condemnation, when purgatory will be abolished and the gates of hell eternally shut: "The sea gave up its dead; then Death and Hades gave up their dead. All the dead were judged according to their deeds. Then Death and Hades were thrown into the pool of fire. (This pool of fire is the second death.)" (Rv. 20:13-14). And this "second death", we know, has no power over those who have taken part in the first resurrection: "Blessed and holy is the one who shares in the first resurrection. The second death has no power over these..." (Rv. 20:6).

That the first instance of judgment is "General", is

confirmed by the established premise that Christ will indeed judge *all* the living that have received the mark of the beast, whereby he might purify the earth of all evil. While this first instance is rightly considered a General Judgment of the living who have not observed God's commandments, Christ will not, for that matter, descend "in the flesh" nor pronounce judgment "publicly", as he will in the case of the second instance of the General Judgment of *all* the dead. Rather, many will die and undergo their particular judgment during the first tribulation, the chief purpose of which will be that of purifying the earth of all evil.

God will not, for that matter, call to judgment only those souls who have incurred his wrath, but also the good who were martyred during those days. "Each of the martyrs was given a long white robe, and they were told to be patient a little while longer until the quota was filled of their fellow servants and brothers to be slain, as they had been" (cf. Rv. 6:11). Needless to say, both the good and the bad who die at this time will receive their Particular Judgment. The good survivors of the first tribulation, Zechariah tells us, will constitute but "one-third" of humanity (Zec. 13:8) and shall inherit the earth during the millenary interspace. At the second instance, however, not only will Christ descend in the flesh in the sight of all and pronounce publicly the sentences of condemnation and righteousness, but will conclude human history by definitively separating the sheep from the goats.

2. Second Instance of Christ's General Judgment

The following characteristics are peculiar to the second instance:

God *the Father is seated with his Son on the throne, judgment comes by fire* and is of *the dead* (Rv. 20:12-13):

a. A Judgment by Way of the Son Who Is Seated at

the Right Hand of the Father's Throne and With Fire

"Thrones were set up and the Ancient One took his throne. His clothing was snow white, and the hair on his head as white as wool; His throne was flames of *fire*, with wheels of burning *fire*. A surging stream of *fire* flowed out from where he sat... The court was convened, and the *books were opened*" (Dn. 7:9-10).

"I saw one like a son of man coming, on the clouds of heaven; when he reached the Ancient One... he received dominion, glory, and kingship; nations and peoples of every language serve him. His dominion is an everlasting dominion..." (Dn. 7:13-14).

"And the day that is coming will set them on *fire*, leaving them neither root nor branch, says the Lord of hosts" (Mal. 3:19).

"When the Son of Man comes in glory, and all the angels with him, *he will sit upon his glorious throne*, and all the nations will be assembled before him. And he will separate them one from another, as a shepherd separates the sheep from the goats..." (Mt. 25:31-33).

"Nor does the Father judge anyone, but he has given all judgment to his Son..." (Jn. 5:22).

"...the work of each will come to light, for the Day will disclose it. It will be revealed with *fire*, and the *fire* itself will test the quality of each one's work" (1 Cor. 3:13).

"For the sake of the joy that lay before him, he endured the Cross, despising its shame, and *has taken his seat at the right of the throne of God*" (Heb. 12:2).

"But *fire* came down from heaven and consumed them [the Devil, Gog and his followers]... *I saw the dead, the great and the lowly, standing before the throne, and scrolls were opened. Then another scroll was opened, the book of life. The dead were judged according to their deeds..."* (Rv. 20:9-13).

"To announce... his time has come *to sit in judgment"* (Rv. 14:6, 7).

b. A Judgment by Way of Fire and the Heavens and Earth are Dissolved

"The Lord is king, let the earth rejoice... Cloud and darkness surround the Lord; justice and right are the foundation of his throne. *Fire* goes before him; *everywhere it consumes the foes.* Lightning illumines the world; the earth sees and trembles. The mountains melt like wax before the Lord, before the Lord of all the earth... *because of your judgments, O Lord... Light dawns for the just,* gladness for the honest of heart. Rejoice in the Lord, you just and praise his holy name" (Ps. 97).

"The heavens shall be rolled up: like a scroll..." (Is. 34:4).

"When you walk through the *fire,* you shall not be burned; the flames shall not consume you" (Is. 43:2).

"...the heavens grow thin like smoke, the earth wears out like a garment" (Is. 51.6).

"When in the *fire* of his jealousy all the earth shall be consumed" (Zep. 1:18).

"...in the *fire* of my jealousy shall all the earth be consumed" (Zep. 3:8).

"Then the Lord God showed me this: he called for *a judgment by fire"* (Am. 7:4).

"...the heavens will pass away with a mighty roar and the elements will be dissolved *by fire,* and the earth and everything done on it will be found out" (2 Pt. 3:10).

"But *fire* came down from heaven and consumed them" (Rv. 20:9).

c. Then There Were Permanent New Heavens and New Earth

"Lo, I am about to create new heavens and a new earth" (Is. 65:17).

"...we await new heavens and a new earth" (2 Pt. 3:13).

"Then I saw a new heaven and a new earth. The former heaven and the former earth had passed away..." (Rv. 21:1).

d. A Judgment of All the Dead — Not Simply of the Living, Nor by the Sword

"...resurrection of *the dead*" (Heb. 6:2).

"*The dead* were judged according to their deeds..." (Rv. 20:12).

"The final act of judgment is an assizes at which *the dead are judged*" (*Dictionary of the Bible,* Bruce Pub. Co. Milwaukee, 1965, p. 468).

While the emphasis of the second instance of judgment is placed upon the "dead", it also includes those evil ones who are physically alive and have turned to worship Gog at the end of the millennium; they, too, will be judged and receive their Particular and General Judgment. It appears, however, that these judgments will not be concomitant. Ezekiel places the *relative* distance of seven months between their Particular and General Judgment: "On that day I will give Gog for his tomb a well-known place in Israel... Gog shall be buried there and all his horde... To purify the land, the house of Israel shall need seven months to bury them. All the people of the land shall bury them...*when I reveal my glory,* says the Lord" (Ez. 39:11-13). It is the consistent teaching throughout Scripture that Gog represents Satan's last reprisal. Furthermore, since the General Resurrection is the eternal rejoining of all bodies to their respective souls, the seven months of burying "bodies" will necessarily precede the General Judgment.

In demonstrating the nature of the millennium as contained in our three sources — Sacred Scripture, Tradition and the Magisterium — we are accorded a certain additional value as far as the doctrines on the temporary kingdom, or true millennium are concerned. By way of Tradition, the Fathers carefully conveyed their teaching on a temporal kingdom. Much more than a simple explanation of formal biblical revelation, their teaching possesses strong ties to the revelation of the Apostles.

Peter, Paul, John, Matthew, and many of the Old Testament writers attest to the permanence of a theology on the millennium, and the General Judgment. The characteristics contained in these doctrines, which we shall now examine in greater depth, were not invented as some like to think, but transmitted by Christ himself, developed by the early Fathers, and sanctified by Holy Mother Church. These doctrines provide ample proof which attests to their life-history — a "living tradition" that maintains a continuity and homogeneity with the doctrines of the Apostles.

As we have seen, the two instances constitute just one General Judgment; they respectively culminate with the transformation of time and the end of human history. Inasmuch as the two instances comprise one judgment, the two kingdoms to follow comprise one heavenly city on earth, the former being the temporal kingdom, a prelude to the eternal and definitively established kingdom of the New Jerusalem. Although we may use the word "kingdom" to describe the paradisal state of both the era of peace and the heavenly Jerusalem, they are nonetheless unique, as both possess nuances peculiar to their duration.

Cited below are, once again, the three sources that formulate our Catholic doctrine: Sacred Scripture, Tradition and the Magisterium. Each describes unequivocal characteristics of the two kingdoms we have addressed. Since it is the chief mission of the Magisterium to keep and preserve the deposit of faith that comes to us from the Apostles (*kèrygma ton apostolon*), we herein appeal to the faith of the Church as our sole criterion. This consequently affords all truth-seeking Catholics the assurance of filial obedience to that Divine Agent who guides her to the truth in all things.

CHAPTER 5

CHARACTERISTICS OF THE TEMPORAL KINGDOM

The following characteristics pertain to that period within human history as they are referenced in Sacred Scripture, Tradition and Magisterial pronouncements. The concepts of the temporal kingdom — that is, "the millennium", "a Sabbath", "a thousand years", "an era", "an age to come", etc. — should now appear more prominent in the deposit of faith. Gradually, the walls of doctrinal division that separated *millenarianism* from the existence of a *temporal kingdom* should become easier to identify as these three sources of our faith aid in clarifying the misty ambiguities that have for too long clouded the minds of many Christians.

In presenting the following characteristics of the temporary kingdom, therefore, quotations from all three sources are provided. I have chosen to refrain as much as possible from superfluous comments due to the proper respect these unmodified doctrines deserve. Their pedagogy, rich as it is, stands on its own merit.

1.1. Times of Refreshment

"Repent, therefore, and be converted, that your sins may

be wiped away, and that the Lord may grant you *times of refreshment* and send you the Messiah already appointed for you, Jesus, whom heaven must receive *until* the times of universal restoration of which God spoke through the mouth of his holy prophets from of old" (Acts 3:19-21).

Reminiscent of the aforementioned quotation, we recall Tertullian: "We say that this city has been provided by God for receiving the saints on their resurrection, and *refreshing them* with the abundance of all really spiritual blessings" (Adversus Marcion, *Ibid.*).

Here we have two separate instances: 1) times of refreshment: the Millennium; 2) the times of universal restoration: the New Jerusalem. There are many other traces of the "times" of refreshment in Scripture, such as:

"...judgment was pronounced in favor of the holy ones of the Most High, and the *time* came when the holy ones possessed the kingdom" (Dn. 7:22).

"Before you are judged, seek merit for yourself, and at *the time of visitation* you will have a ransom" (Sir. 18:19).

"Therefore upon the idols of the nations shall *a visitation* come..." (Wis. 14:11).

"For it is the seedtime of peace" (Zec. 8:12).

"The Lord of hosts will *visit* his flock" [not "dwell for ever and ever"] (Zec. 10:3).

N.B. Here the inspired author employs the term "visit" or "visitation", as opposed to the word "dwell", which is used in Scripture primarily to signify an ongoing, eternal dwelling. These three passages do not treat the concept of "time", according to our estimation, but within the context of a "transformed" world, whose duration is known only to God.

"...this is what was spoken through the prophet Joel: 'It

will come to pass in the last days,' God says, 'that I will pour out a portion of my Spirit upon all flesh. Your sons and your daughters shall prophesy, your young men shall see visions, your old men shall dream dreams. Indeed, upon my servants and my handmaids I will pour out a portion of my spirit in those days, and they shall prophesy...' " (Acts 2:16-18). The Spirit's dynamic presence mentioned here recalls the words of the prophet Ezekiel: "I will give you a new heart and place a new Spirit within you, taking from your body your stony hearts and giving you natural hearts. I will put my Spirit within you and make you live by my statutes, careful to observe my decrees" (Ez. 36:26-27).

"Then the disciples asked him, 'Why do the scribes say that Elijah must come first?' He said in reply, 'Elijah will indeed come and restore all things...'" (Mt. 17:10-11). The Fathers concur that Elijah will come at the time of Antichrist.

1.2.   Sabbath Rest; the Seventh Day

"'And He rested on the seventh day.' This means: *when His Son will come and destroy the time of the lawless one and judge the godless, and change the sun and the moon and the stars — then He shall indeed rest on the seventh day...* You see what He means... that Sabbath which I have made, in which, after giving rest to all things, I will make the beginning of the eighth day, that is, the beginning of another world" (Letter of Barnabas, *Ibid.*).

"Now... we understand that a period of one thousand years is indicated in symbolic language. When it was said of Adam that 'in the day that he eateth of the tree, in that he shall die,' we knew he was not a thousand years old [Adam lived to be 963]. We also believe that the words, 'The day of the Lord is a thousand years', also led some to the same conclusion. Moreover, a man among us named John, one of Christ's

Apostles, received and foretold that *the followers of Christ would dwell in Jerusalem for a thousand years,* and that afterwards the universal and, in short, everlasting resurrection and judgment would take place" (Dialogue with Trypho, *Ibid.*).

"Since all the works of God were completed in six days, the world must continue in its present state through six ages, that is, six thousand years. For the great Day of God is limited by a circle of *a thousand years,* as the prophet shows, who says (Ps. 90:4), 'A thousand years in your eyes are merely a yesterday.' And as God labored during those six days in creating such great works, so His religion and truth must labor during these six thousand years, while wickedness prevails and bears rule. And again, since God, having finished His works, rested on the seventh day and blessed it, at the end of the six thousandth year all wickedness must be abolished from the earth, and righteousness reign for *a thousand years*; and there must be tranquility and *rest* from the labors which the world now long has endured" (The Divine Institutes, *Ibid.*).

"Scripture says: 'And God rested upon the seventh day from all His works'... And in six days created things were completed; it is evident, therefore, that they will come to an end at the sixth thousand year... But when the Antichrist shall have devastated all things in this world, he will reign for three years and six months, and sit in the temple at Jerusalem; and then the Lord will come from Heaven in the clouds... sending this man and those who follow him into the lake of fire; but bringing in for the righteous the times of the kingdom, that is, the rest, the hallowed seventh day... These are to take place in *the times of the kingdom,* that is, upon the seventh day... the true Sabbath of the righteous" (Adversus Haereses, *Ibid.*, Bk. 28, Ch. 3; Bk. 30,4; Bk. 33,2).

"The saints should thus enjoy a kind of Sabbath-rest during that period, a holy leisure after the labors of six thousand years since man was created...(and) there should follow on the completion of six thousand years, as of six days, a kind of seventh-day Sabbath in the succeeding thousand years; and that it is for this purpose the saints rise, *viz.*, to celebrate this Sabbath. And this opinion would not be objectionable, if it were believed that the joys of the saints, in that Sabbath shall be spiritual..." (*De Civitate Dei, Ibid.*).

"Your vindication shall go *before* you, and the glory of the Lord shall be your *rear* guard..." [vindication precedes glory] (Is. 58:8).

"Here comes with power the Lord God... his recompense *before* him" (Is. 40:10). Vindicating and recompensing "before" are allusive of that which we have identified as the first tribulation and the Sabbath rest, which precede the eternal kingdom of the New Jerusalem brought about by the glorious manifestation of the Redeemer which constitutes their "rear guard".

"For we who believed enter into that rest... For he has somewhere spoken about the seventh day in this manner, 'And God rested on the seventh day from all his works'; and again... 'They shall not enter into my rest'. Therefore... it remains that some will enter into it... a Sabbath rest still remains for the people of God. And whoever enters into God's rest, rests from his own works as God did from his. Therefore, let us strive to enter into that rest..." (Heb. 4:3-6, 9-11).

1.3. First Resurrection

St. John's Revelation speaks of a first resurrection of those who had been beheaded during the reign of Antichrist. These came back to life and reigned for a thousand years, or for a *Day* during the "millenary interspace": "Blessed and holy is the one who shares in the first resurrection. The second death has no power over these; they will be priests of God and of Christ and they will reign with him for a thousand years" (Rv. 20:6). The Apostolic Tradition bears witness to these "priests of

God" who experience a first resurrection.

"But *I and every other orthodox Christian feel certain that there will be a resurrection of the flesh, followed by a thousand years* in the rebuilt, embellished, and enlarged city of Jerusalem, as was announced by the Prophets Ezekiel, Isaias and others" (Dialogue with Trypho, *Ibid.*).

"The Lord Himself says, 'As Jonah remained *three days and three nights* in the whale's belly, so shall the Son of man be in the heart of the earth... If, then, the Lord observed the law of the dead... how must these men be put to confusion, who allege that... [at the Millennium] the inner man, leaving the body here, ascends into the super celestial place?... It is manifest that the souls of his disciples also, upon whose account the Lord underwent these things, shall go away into the invisible place allotted to them by God, and there remain until the [first] resurrection, awaiting *that* event, and rising in their entirety, that is, in their entirety j*ust as the Lord arose* [with a glorified, spiritual body with which he passed through the cenacle doors], they shall come into the presence of God... For the *new flesh* which rises up again is the same which receives the *new cup"* [cf. Mt. 26:27] (Adversus Haereses, *Ibid.*, Bk. 31, Ch. 1-2; 33,1).

N.B. Whenever the word "presence" is mentioned by Father Irenaeus, it is meant to convey not an earthly reign of Christ in the flesh, but a reign of his physical presence in the Eucharist reverenced and worshiped by those who have risen.

"So, the blessing foretold undoubtedly refers to the time of His Kingdom, when *the just will rule on rising from the dead"* (Adversus Haereses, *Ibid.*).

"We say that this city has been provided by God for receiving the saints on their resurrection, and refreshing them with the abundance of all really spiritual blessings... We do confess that a kingdom is promised to us upon the earth, although before heaven, only in another state of existence;

inasmuch as it will be *after the resurrection for a thousand years* in the divinely-built city of Jerusalem..." (Adversus Marcion, *Ibid.*).

"But He, when He shall have destroyed unrighteousness, and executed His great judgment, and *shall have recalled to life* the righteous, who have lived from the beginning, will be engaged among men a thousand years, and will rule them with most just command... Then they who *shall be alive in their bodies* shall not die" (The Divine Institutes, *Ibid.*).

N.B. As mentioned earlier, Christ will be engaged among men in the Eucharist, not in the flesh.

And last but not least, to give impetus to this doctrine of the first resurrection, the ordinary Magisterium states that *"all the just who live during this time have a first resurrection..."* (*The Faith Explained, Ibid.*).

"Some Catholic Scholars believe that the 'thousand years' is a figure of speech for a long period of time before the end of the world, when the Church will enjoy a great peace and Christ will reign *over* the souls of men. All the just who live during this time have a first resurrection..." (*Ibid.*).

"They [those who had been beheaded for their witness to Jesus] came to life and they reigned with Christ for a thousand years... This is the first resurrection. Blessed and holy is the one who shares in the first resurrection. The second death has no power over these..." (Rv. 20:4-6).

1.4. The Remnant of the Millennium

"A man among us named John, one of Christ's Apostles, received and foretold that *the followers of Christ would dwell in Jerusalem for a thousand years,* and that afterwards the universal and, in short, everlasting resurrection and judgment would take place" (Dialogue with Trypho, *Ibid.*).

"The poor will possess the land... those blessed by the Lord will possess the land... the just will possess the land and live in it forever" (passim Ps. 37).

"My chosen ones shall inherit the land" (Is. 65:9).

"The coast shall belong to the remnant of the house of Judah... for the Lord their God shall *visit* them and bring about their *restoration*" (Zep. 2:7).

"Blessed are the meek, for they will inherit the land" (Mt. 5:5).

"They have been *ransomed* as the *first fruits* of the human race..." (Rv. 14:4).

1.5. Evil Abolished for a Time

"It is fitting, therefore, that creation itself, being restored to its primeval condition, should without restraint be under the dominion of the righteous... And it is right that when creation is restored, all the animals should obey and be in subjection to man, and revert to the food originally given by God... that is, the productions of the earth (Adversus Haereses, *Ibid.*, Bk. 32, Ch. 1; 33, 4).

"But the poor from the edge of the sword and from the hand of the mighty he saves... Out of six troubles he will deliver you, and at the *seventh* no evil shall touch you... the beasts of the earth you need not dread. You shall be in league with the stones of the field and the wild beasts shall be at peace with you" (Jb. 5:15-23).

"At the end of the six thousandth year all wickedness must be abolished from the earth, and righteousness reign for *a thousand years"* (The Divine Institutes, *Ibid.*).

"On that day the Lord will punish... the kings of the earth on the earth. They will be gathered together like prisoners into a pit; they will be shut up in a dungeon, and after many days they will be punished..." (Is. 24:21, 22).

"All who are alert to do evil will be cut off..." (Is. 29:20).

"A highway will be there, called the holy way. No one unclean may pass over it... It is for those with a journey to make..." (Is. 35:8-9).

"In justice shall you be established, far from the fear of oppression..." (Is. 54:14).

"My chosen ones shall inherit the land... Sharon shall be a pasture for the flocks and the valley of Achor a resting place for cattle of my people who have sought me. But you who forsake me... you I will destine for the sword" (Is. 65:9-12).

"He seized the dragon, the ancient serpent, which is the Devil or Satan, and tied it up for a thousand years... so that it could no longer lead the nations astray until the thousand years are completed. After this, it is to be released for a short time" (Rv. 20:2-3).

1.6.   Procreation to a Long Life Span

"There shall no more be an infant of days there, nor an old man that shall not fill up his days; for the child shall die a hundred years old... For as the days of the tree of life, so shall be the days of My people, and the works of their hands shall be multiplied. My elect shall not labor in vain, nor bring forth children for a curse; for they shall be a righteous seed blessed by the Lord, and their posterity with them" (Dialogue with

Trypho, *Ibid.*).

"Also there shall not be any immature one, nor an old man who does not fulfill his time; for the youth shall be of a hundred years old..." (Adversus Haereses, *Ibid.*, Bk. 34, Ch. 4).

"You shall know that your descendants are many, and your offspring as the grass of the earth. You shall approach the grave in full vigor, as a shock of grain comes in at its season" (Jb. 5:25-26).

"They who shall be alive in their bodies shall not die, but during those thousand years shall produce an infinite multitude, and their offspring shall be holy and beloved by God..." (The Divine Institutes, *Ibid.*).

"Raise a glad cry, you barren one who did not bear, break forth in jubilant song, you who were not in labor, for more numerous are the children of the deserted wife than the children of her who has a husband..." (Is. 54:1).

"I will give them recompense faithfully, a lasting covenant I will make with them. Their descendants shall be renowned among the nations, and their offspring among the peoples" (Is. 61:8-9).

"As the years of a tree, so the years of my people... They shall not toil in vain nor beget children for sudden destruction; for a race blessed by the Lord are they and their offspring" (Is. 65:22-23).

"Behold, I will gather them together from all the lands to which in anger, wrath and great rage I banished them; I will bring them back to this place and settle them here in safety... One heart and one way I will give them, that they may fear me always, to their own good and that of their children after them" (Jer. 32:37-39).

"See, I come to you... I will settle crowds of men upon

you... cities shall be repeopled, and ruins rebuilt. I will settle crowds of men and beasts upon you, to multiply and be fruitful. I will repeople you as in the past, and be more generous to you than in the beginning; thus you shall know that I am the Lord" (Ez. 36:9-11).

"I will make them not few, but many... His sons shall be as of old, his assembly before me shall stand firm" (Jer. 30:19-20).

"Old men and old women, each with staff in hand because of old age, shall again sit in the streets of Jerusalem. The city shall be filled with boys and girls playing in her streets... I will whistle for them to come together and when I redeem them they will be as numerous as before" (Zec. 8:4-5; 10:8).

1.7. Terrestrial Paradise

a. Earth and All Creation will Rejoice

"He will change the sun and the moon and the stars" (Letter of Barnabas, *Ibid.*).

"Creation, reborn and freed from bondage, will yield an abundance of food of all kind from the heaven's dew and the fertility of the earth" (Adversus Haereses, *Ibid.*).

"At the end of the six thousandth year all wickedness must be abolished from the earth, and righteousness reign for a thousand years" (The Divine Institutes, *Ibid.*).

"The earth will open its fruitfulness and bring forth most abundant fruits of its own accord; the rocky mountains shall drip with honey; streams of wine shall run down, and rivers flow with milk; in short the world itself shall rejoice, and all nature exult, being rescued and set free from the dominion of evil and impiety, and guilt and error" (The Divine Institutes, *Ibid.*).

b. Laboring and Replenishing, but Not in Vain

"And they shall build houses and inhabit them; and they shall plant vineyards, and eat the fruits of them, and drink the wine... and the works of their hands shall be multiplied. My elect shall not labor in vain" (Dialogue with Trypho, *Ibid.*).

"The earth shall yield its fruit, for God, our God, has blessed us" (cf. Ps. 67:7).

"...that the mountains may yield their bounty for the people, and the hills great abundance..." (Ps. 72:3).

"He will give rain for the seed that you sow in the ground, and the wheat that the soil produces shall be rich and abundant. On that Day your cattle will graze in spacious meadows; the oxen and the asses that till the ground will eat silage tossed to them with shovel and pitchfork. Upon every high mountain and lofty hill there will be streams of running water" (Is. 30:23-25).

"...the earth brings forth its plants and a garden makes its growth spring up..." (Is. 61:11).

"They shall live in the houses they build, and eat the fruit of the vineyards they plant... and my chosen ones shall long enjoy the produce of their hands. They shall not toil in vain" (Is. 65:21-23).

"I will prepare for them peaceful fields for planting..." (Ez. 34:29).

"See, I come to you... you will be tilled and sown, and I will settle crowds of men upon you... cities shall be repeopled, and ruins rebuilt" (Ez. 36:9-10).

"The forests and every kind of fragrant tree have overshadowed Israel at God's command, for God *is leading* Israel in joy by the light of his glory..." (Bar. 5:8).

"Again they shall dwell in his shade and raise grain" (Hos. 14:8).

"They shall rebuild and inhabit their ruined cities, plant vineyards and drink the wine, set out gardens and eat the fruits" (Am. 9:14).

"For it is the seedtime of peace: the vine shall yield its fruit, the land shall bear its crops, and the heavens shall give their dew" (Zec. 8:12).

c. *Like* Eden

"Her deserts he shall make like Eden, her wasteland like the garden of the Lord" (Is. 51:3).

"'This desolate land has been made into a garden of Eden', they shall say" (Ez. 36:35).

1.8.   Christ's Reign *Over* the Earth

Since Jesus' reign in the temporary kingdom will be in his Eucharistic Person, there is no reason to postulate theories of him reigning "in the flesh" on earth. Not only has this notion been condemned by Holy Mother Church, but it contradicts the very purpose of an historic millennium. In order for terrestrial progress to occur within a social order in human history, man must *freely* respond to divine action through his talents and resources.

As long as history endures, the opposing forces of good and evil, grace and sin, will always exist to some degree: "If anyone asserts that this sin of Adam... which is in *all* human beings... can be taken away by the powers of human nature or by any other remedy other than the merits of the one mediator our Lord Jesus Christ who reconciled us with God by his blood... *anathema sit* "(*The Christian Faithful*, Society of St. Paul, 6th Ed., 1995, n. 510); "By the sweat of your face shall you get bread to eat..." (Gn. 3:19). Despite the Devil being enchained during the temporal kingdom, the roots of original sin will remain. Hence, the need for the Sacraments will continue. The three forces which, according to St. John, entice us to sin — namely, the Devil, the flesh and the world — will no longer have power over the saints who inherit this kingdom; the devil, former prince of the world, will be enchained, the world transformed, and its enticements, therefore, extinguished.

Indeed, the three agents of sin will lose their control over the saints who live in these "times of refreshment", "for it was not to angels that he subjected the world *to come*...," but to man, "subjecting all things under his feet" (Heb. 2:5-8). For a time, all will act in perfect accord and harmony with God's Will. Thus, man will work for the common good of society under God's fruitful gaze which bestows abundant graces upon all human endeavors. Man, in turn, by collaborating with God's gratuitous grace, will cause society to advance and progress in holiness. While the earth can yield nothing but that which man has sown, it will, nonetheless, be God who blesses the earth by granting grace to mankind's labors.

Were Christ to reign "in the flesh" on earth, however, not only would it signal the end of human history but also the end of man's toil and labor. At the end of human history, the perpetual sacrifice will also cease, along with a host of other characteristics which the Fathers unanimously agree upon.

The following verses demonstrate that Christ's reign with the saints during the millennium is not to be intended as an earthly reign, that is "on" the earth, but rather a heavenly reign, "over" the earth. This is a crucial distinction that many

Christian denominations have failed to include in their theology.

"These are the words of Isaias concerning the millennium: 'For there shall be a new heaven and a new earth, and the former shall not be remembered... but they shall be glad and rejoice in these things, which I create. For, behold, I make Jerusalem a rejoicing, and my people a joy; and I shall rejoice *over* Jerusalem, and be glad *over* My people'" (Dialogue with Trypho, *Ibid.*).

"But He, when He shall have destroyed unrighteousness... will be *engaged among men* a thousand years" (The Divine Institutes, *Ibid.*).

"The coming of Christ in the second Advent... is the consummation of all things, the end of human history. *If before that final end there is to be a period, more or less prolonged, of triumphant sanctity, such a result will be brought about, not by the apparition of the Person of Christ in Majesty but by the operation of those powers of sanctification which are now at work, the Holy Ghost and the Sacraments of the Church*" (*The Teaching of the Catholic Church: A Summary of Catholic Doctrine, Ibid.*).

"Show yourself over the heavens, God; may your glory appear *above* all the earth" (Ps. 57:6).

"And I shall rejoice *over* Jerusalem, and be glad *over* My people" (Is. 65:19) (from *Septuaginta,* 1d est Vetus Testamentum graece iuxta LXX interpretes; edidit Alfred Rahls; Duo volumina in uno; Deutsche Bibelgesellschaft, Stuttgart, Germany, 1979). Once again, use of the word "over" clearly signifies that Christ will reign not "on" the earth, but from above.

1.9. Jesus' Reign in the Eucharist

"...I will be in the *glory* in her midst" (Zec. 2:9).

"They will not hunger or thirst any more, nor will the sun or any heat strike them. For *the Lamb*, who is the center of the throne, will shepherd them..." (Rv. 7:16).

"The Lamb" in Sacred Scripture is a consistent prefiguration of "the Eucharist", that is, Jesus who offers himself as a holy and unblemished sacrifice to the Father on behalf of sinful humanity. The author of the letter to the Hebrews tells us that Christ is the High Priest who offered himself for us once and for all as God's sacrificial Lamb. Accordingly, the Book of Revelation reiterates Christ's intermediary role between the Father and the human race: "...One hundred forty-four thousand (144,000)...had his name and his Father's name written on their foreheads... These are the ones who follow *the Lamb* wherever he goes... they have been ransomed as the first fruits of the human race..." (Rv. 14:1, 4).

These first fruits of the remnant numbering 144,000 are those who have been ransomed by Christ and will adore him as "the Lamb" (that is, in his Eucharistic presence) wherever he goes. "Wherever he goes" signifies wherever he is present, namely, in all the tabernacles of the world. The Lamb, commonly referred to by St. Paul as "Christ Jesus", is invoked in the Church's liturgical worship under the appearances of bread and wine.

And we know from St. John's Gospel that this bread comes down from heaven and "gives life to the world" (Jn. 6:33). Without the Eucharist, there would be nothing to sustain the earth during this millenary interspace. Christ Jesus, the true Son of God who is the "Light of the world", will banish all darkness from this present earth in order to inaugurate the kingdom of saints and give glory to his heavenly Father. Our reigning Pontiff, Pope John Paul II, referred to the third millennium as a period which will be marked by an intensified

126

devotion to Christ in the Eucharist: "The year 2000 will be intensely Eucharistic" (*Tertio Millennio Adveniente, Ibid.*, 55).

The temporal kingdom, therefore, will have at its core, in the hearts and souls of all its faithful, the glorious Person of Christ Jesus who will shine forth above all in the triumph of his Eucharistic Person. The Eucharist will become the summit of all humanity, extending its rays of light to all the nations. The Eucharistic heart of Jesus, dwelling in their midst, will thus cultivate in the faithful a spirit of intense adoration and worship never before seen. Freed from the deceptions of the contriver, who will be enchained for a time, the faithful will gather around all the tabernacles of the earth to render homage to God — their sustenance, their solace and their salvation.

1.10. Ministerial Priesthood

"I will lavish choice portions upon the priests, and my people will be filled with my blessings, says the Lord" (Jer. 31:14).

"And everywhere they bring sacrifice to my name, and a pure offering, for great is My name among the nations, says the Lord of hosts" (Mal. 1:11).

"But who will endure the day of his coming?... He will purify the sons of Levi [the priestly family], refining them like gold or like silver that they may offer due sacrifice to the Lord. Then the sacrifice of Judah and Jerusalem will please the Lord, as in the days of old..." (Mal. 3:2-4).

"The pots in the house of the Lord shall be as the libation bowls before the altar... And all who come to sacrifice shall take them and cook in them. On that day there shall be no longer any merchant in the house of the Lord of hosts" (Zec. 14:20, 21).

1.11.   Common Priesthood

All shall become priests and repossess the original priestly character which was once ours in the paradisal Garden of Eden.

In Adam and Eve's original state of perfect bliss and union with their Creator, everything existed in perfect submission to the will of their Maker. Sacrifice was offered up with each passing moment — not one of the blood of animals that atones for sin, but a pure and perfect offering of the human will through a sublime act of obedience to the Will of their Creator. Such a sacrifice, as offered in the unblemished original state, was perhaps more a gift than a sacrifice. For Adam and Eve continuously offered perfect praise to God in thanksgiving for all the blessings he had bestowed upon them. As a consequence, they became filled with a total trust and ardent desire to cling to the Will of their maker, who provided them with all that was necessary for their perpetual state of eternal bliss. In this offering of their free will to God in the garden of Eden, we discover the original character of the *priesthood*: "...every high priest is appointed to offer *gifts* and sacrifices" (Heb. 8:3).

Sin did not enter into the economy of God's creation until Adam's fall. Once Adam voluntarily juxtaposed his own will with that of his Creator, division entered the world, whereby he and his partner were removed from the Garden and stripped of their preternatural gifts. From this expulsion, Adam and Eve's priesthood underwent a radical change in character; sacrifice was no longer a largesse or a free offering of praise, but also one of atonement. Sacrifice eventually became an offering of "the blood of goats and bulls" (Heb. 9:13) in atonement for the sin and division that had entered the world. Only through a gradual reordering of a fallen world did sin and division become reversible and once and for all conquerable. Jesus, above and outside the fallen world in a paradisal state of innocence similar to that of Adam and Eve before the fall, was the first fruit of its reordering.

By becoming like us, Jesus reproduced the perfect state of innocence in which a pure sacrifice of praise was offered through the perfect submission of the human will to the Father: "...I do not seek my own will but the Will of the One who sent me" (Jn. 5:30). By assuming the frailty of our human condition, he "learned obedience from what he suffered" (Heb. 5:8), that is, the obedience once offered by Adam and Eve. Hence, Jesus' pure sacrifice, unlike those of the high priests who "offer sacrifice day after day" (Heb. 7:27), was founded upon "a new covenant" of which he is the mediator (Heb. 9:15). "When he speaks of a 'new' covenant, he declares the old one obsolete" (Heb. 8:13). Where a sacrifice is offered in his memory, there is no invention of atonement for sins, for Jesus "did that once for all when he offered himself" (Heb. 7:27). This new covenant, ratified and consummated through the blood of Christ, had for its scope a pledge of future glory in which the world's reordering should come through the primacy of spirit and love. The perpetuation of unbloodied sacrifices of Christ at Holy Mass, celebrated in love and thanksgiving to the Father through the Son and in the Holy Spirit, have as their objective the world's renewal as it groans in anxious expectation. Indeed, responding to his disciples' petition that he teach them how to pray, Jesus reminds us: "Our Father... thy kingdom come, *thy will be done on earth* as it is in heaven..." (cf. Mt. 6:10).

By evading the Will of the heavenly Father, mankind had erected and reinforced the walls of division that separate us from God. But in virtue of Christ's total submission to the Will of his heavenly Father, these walls of division began to crumble one by one. Jesus, whose mission it was to reconcile all things to himself and to the Father, demonstrated his saving powers as a man outside the world of sin by mastering the laws of nature: calming the tempestuous winds, walking on the waters, curing the lame, healing the deaf, giving sight to the blind, etc. By this means, Jesus inaugurated the reordering of the world, the reign of God's Will on earth.

By coming into the world through a virginal birth, Christ became the new standard for the relationship between nature and grace. As the new Adam, born of the new Eve, he bound the laws of nature and grace and thus began the process of restoration to the origins of the world's creation. This process of liberating nature from its divisions continues daily in the perpetual Holy Sacrifice of the Mass, and is spurred on by the holiness of the members of Christ's mystical body, the Church. While these cogs of the divine mechanism combine to "fill up the sufferings that are lacking in the passion of Christ for the sake of his body, the Church" (cf. Col. 1:24), they gradually discover their ultimate meaning in obedience to God's Will — that same obedience Adam and Eve once lived, but of which Christ has now made us co-heirs, adopted sons.

Christians, Paul states, are "...predestined to be conformed to the image of his Son, so that he might be the firstborn among many brothers" (Rom. 8:29). Thus, even "though we bear the image of the earthly one, we shall also bear the image of the heavenly one" (1 Cor. 15:49).

This heavenly image, impressed upon all Christians in virtue of their baptismal consecration, makes them participants in Christ's priestly office. Vatican II spoke of the two types of priesthood that are exercised by all the Christian faithful:

> Though they differ essentially and not only in degree, the common priesthood of the faithful and the ministerial or hierarchical priesthood are nonetheless ordered one to another; each in its own proper way shares in the one priesthood of Christ. The ministerial priest, by the sacred power that he has... effects the Eucharistic sacrifice and offers it to God in the name of all the people. The faithful indeed, by virtue of their royal priesthood, participate in the offering of the Eucharist. They exercise that priesthood too, by the reception of the sacraments, prayer and

thanksgiving, by the witness of a holy life, abnegation and active charity" (*Lumen Gentium*, *Ibid.*, n. 10).

Both the ministerial and the royal priesthood are ordered to function within the Church, by means of the Church and for the good of the Church, but after the second instance of General Judgment, this twofold character will change: "For as often as you eat this bread and drink the cup, you proclaim the death of the Lord *until* he comes" (1 Cor. 11:26); "I am with you always, *until* the end of the age" (Mt. 28:20). When Christ comes in the flesh at the end of human history, there will no longer be the need for the daily offering of our Lord's body and blood at Mass: "Until there is realized new heavens and new earth...the pilgrim Church, in her Sacraments and institutions, *which belong to this present age, carry the mark of this world which will pass...*" (*CCC, Ibid.*, 671). However, freed from the bonds of sin and division during the Millennium, the original priestly character, a gift from the Spirit, will once again enable the earth's inhabitants to worship in spirit and truth, thereby reflecting the image of the heavenly one in creation:

"You yourselves shall be named priests of the Lord, ministers of our God you shall be called" (Is. 61:6).

"...like living stones, let yourselves be built up into a spiritual house to be a holy priesthood to offer spiritual sacrifices acceptable to God through Jesus Christ" (1 Pt. 2:5).

"...you are 'a chosen race, a royal priesthood, a holy nation, a people of his own, so that you may announce the praises' of him who called you out of darkness into his wonderful light" (1 Pt. 2:9).

"You made them a kingdom and priests for our God, and they will reign on earth" (Rv. 5:10).

"Blessed and holy is the one who shares in the first resurrection. The second death has no power over these; they will be priests of God and of Christ and they will reign with him for the thousand years" (Rv. 20:6).

1.12. Pacific Qualities Such as Abiding Justice, Mercy, Faithfulness and Peace

"We will be made *just* and holy" (Letter of Barnabas, *Ibid.*).

"So, the blessing foretold undoubtedly refers to the time of His Kingdom, when *the just will rule* on rising from the dead" (Adversus Haereses, *Ibid.*).

"Mercy and faithfulness have met, justice and peace have embraced. Faithfulness shall spring from the earth and justice look down from heaven" (cf. Ps. 85:11-12).

"Justice shall be the band around his waist, and faithfulness a belt upon his hips" (Is. 11:5).

"A strong city have we... Open the gates and let in a nation that is *just,* one that keeps *faith.* A nation of firm purpose you keep in *peace*; in peace, for its *trust* in you... When your judgment dawns upon the earth, the world's inhabitants learn justice" (Is. 26:1-3, 9).

1.13. Peace and Harmony

"'The wolves and lambs feed together, and the lion shall eat like the ox, and the serpent shall eat earth like bread. They shall not hurt nor destroy on my holy mountain, saith the Lord...'" [Is. 65:17-25] (Dialogue with Trypho, *Ibid.*).

"All the animals who use the products of the soil will be *at peace and in harmony* with one another, completely at man's beck and call" (Adversus Haereses, *Ibid.*).

"At the end of the six thousandth year, all wickedness must be abolished from the earth, and righteousness reign for a thousand years; and there must be *tranquility* and rest from the labors which the world now long has endured... Throughout this time beasts shall not be nourished by blood, nor birds by prey; but all things shall be *peaceful and tranquil"* (The Divine Institutes, *Ibid.*).

"Then the wolf shall be a guest of the lamb, and the leopard shall lie down with the kid; the calf and the young lion shall browse together, with a little child to guide them. The cow and the bear shall be neighbors, together their young shall rest; the lion shall eat hay like the ox. The baby shall play by the cobra's den, and the child lay his hand on the adder's lair. There shall be no harm or ruin on my holy mountain..." (Is. 11:6-9).

a. No Sorrow or Mourning

"No longer shall the sound of weeping be heard there, or the sound of crying" (Is. 65:19).

"I will turn their mourning into joy, I will console and gladden them after their sorrows. I will lavish choice portions upon the priests, and my people shall be filled with my blessings, says the Lord" (Jer. 31:13, 14).

1.14. Physical Rejuvenation

"They that hope in the Lord will renew their strength, they will soar with eagles' wings, they will run and not grow weary, walk and not grow faint" (Is. 40:31).

"He [the Lord] will renew your strength and you shall be like watered gardens" (Is. 58:11).

"Your youth is renewed like the eagle's" (Ps. 103:5).

"God, my Lord, is my strength; he makes my feet swift as those of hinds and enables me to go upon the heights" (Hb. 3:19).

"...the weakling among them shall be like David on that day" (Zec. 12:8).

1.15. No Illness

"Strengthen the hands that are feeble, make firm the knees that are weak... Then will the eyes of the blind be opened, the ears of the deaf be cleared; Then the lame will leap like a stag, then the tongue of the dumb will sing" (Is. 35:3.5-6);

"I will lead the blind on their journey... I will turn darkness into light before them, and make crooked ways straight" (Is. 42:16).

1.16. Different Tongues

"I come to gather nations of every language; they shall come and see my glory" (Is. 66:18).

"...in those days ten men of every nation, speaking in different tongues, shall take hold, yes, take hold of every Jew by the edge of his garment and say, 'Let us go with you, for we have heard that God is with you'" (Zec. 8:23).

1.17. Instructing and Announcing

"Then the Lord's name will be declared on Zion, the praise of God in Jerusalem, when all peoples and kingdoms gather to worship the Lord" (Ps. 102:22-23).

"Until he establishes justice on the earth, the coastlands will wait for his teaching" (Is. 42:4).

"...the people whom I formed for myself that they might *announce* my praise" (Is. 43:21).

"Publish it to the *ends of the earth* and say, 'The Lord has ransomed his servant Jacob'" (Is. 48:20).

"I will make you a light to the nations that my salvation may reach to the *ends of the earth*" (Is. 49:6).

"So shall your rule be known upon the earth, your saving power among all the nations" (Ps. 67:3).

1.18. Increased Light

"He will change the sun and the moon and the stars" (Letter of Barnabas, *Ibid.*).

"The sun will become seven times brighter than it is now" (The Divine Institutes, *Ibid.*).

"The light of the moon will be like that of the sun and the light of the sun will be seven times greater..." (Is. 30:26).

"I will turn darkness into light before them" (Is. 42:16).

"From one new moon to another, and from one Sabbath to another, all mankind shall come to worship before me, says the Lord" (Is. 66:23).

"Then the righteous will shine like the sun in the kingdom of their Father. Whoever has ears ought to hear" (Mt. 13:43).

1.19. Divine Will on Earth

"Remember the former age, for I am God and there is no god beside, neither is there the like to me: Who show from the beginning the things that shall be at last, and from ancient times the things that as yet are not done, saying: my counsel shall stand, and all my Will shall be done" (cf. Is. 46:8-11).

"I will put my spirit within you and make you live by my statutes, careful to observe my decrees" (Ez. 36:27).

"Your Kingdom come, your Will be done on earth as in heaven" (Mt. 6:10; Lk. 11:2).

"...he has made known to us the mystery of his will in accord with his favor that he set forth in him as a plan for the fullness of times, to sum up all things in Christ, in heaven and on earth" (Eph. 1:9-10).

"Therefore, from the day we heard this, we do not cease praying for you and asking that you may be filled with the knowledge of his will through all spiritual wisdom and understanding... giving thanks to the Father, who has made you fit to share the inheritance of the holy ones in light" (Col. 1:9.12).

"Whoever does the will of God remains into the age" (1 Jn. 2:17) (from *The New Greek-English New Testament*, Tyndale House Publishers, Wheaton, IL, 1990).

1.20. The Day of the Lord

In light of this foretold era or temporary kingdom, the Apostolic Fathers specify the period in which this holy age is to take place, namely after the first tribulation of Antichrist, but before the final tribulation of Satan. Unanimous in their interpretation of Revelation chapters 19 and 20, the Fathers concur on the doctrine of Antichrist preceding the glorious reign of the saints on earth. They constitute these two events of the defeat of Antichrist and the final defeat of Satan as the "Day of the Lord". And just as a day has a beginning, a summit and an end, so this "Day" will dawn and reach its zenith before setting.

As we will be examining the two tribulations, as well as triumphs that respectively precede and culminate in the millennium and the New Jerusalem, it here suffices to refer to the "Day of the Lord" as that great triumph of God over Antichrist, and then Satan. With regard to its application to the first tribulation and triumph, this Day's dawning marks Christ's descent to earth by way of his glorified Spirit. It will be occasioned by a false peace and is commensurate to the first instance of that great and terrible day of the General Judgment of all *the living*. This Day's summit then shifts to the great but temporary kingdom in which God rests with his saints after all his labors. It is occasioned by the sun and moon's increase in intensity of light, such that all darkness will be abolished. And it is here where we encounter what the Fathers have unanimously termed "the Sabbath Rest", a "Seventh Day", used in reference to the six days of creation, after which, on the seventh day, God rested from all his labors. After this rest, the Day will set when "Satan will be released from prison" and "surround the camp of the holy ones and the beloved city" (Rv. 20:7-9). Once this unchaining of the "contriver" takes place, God will wage his final triumphant battle against Satan.

At this point, we come to the second or Great Tribulation and triumph that culminates in the New Jerusalem. This Day will also have a beginning and a summit, but absolutely no end. Its dawn is marked by the cosmic upheavals such as the world has never before seen nor will ever see again. These tribulations have been likened to the labor pangs of a woman who is about to give birth to a "New" creation, to the "New heavens and New earth". Not only is this dawning of the New and eternal Day of the Lord occasioned by the end of human history, but also by the summoning of all mankind to the judgment seat for the great General Judgment of all *the dead*. The Fathers refer to this day as the "Eighth Day", the "Great Feast of Tabernacles" (with "tabernacles" implying our resurrected bodies – cf. The Symposium, *Ibid.*).

Although there are two tribulations and triumphs, they both constitute "the Day of the Lord". These two events are evidenced throughout Scripture and couched in the following expressions:

The Day's Beginning (First Tribulation)

"For you yourselves know very well that *the Day of the Lord* will come like a thief at night" (1 Thes. 5:2).

"With regard to the coming of the Lord Jesus Christ... *that Day* will not come, unless the rebellion comes first, the man of lawlessness...whom the Lord Jesus will kill with the breath of his mouth and render powerless by the manifestation of his coming" (cf. 2 Thes. 2:1-8).

The Day's Peak and End (First Triumph)

"The hour is coming when I will no longer speak to you in figures but I will tell you clearly about the Father. *On that Day* you will ask in my name..." (Jn. 16:25-26). This text alludes to the words of the prophet Isaiah as interpreted by St. Justin Martyr: "'*And it shall come to pass that before they call, I will hear*... Then the wolves and lambs feed together, and the lion shall eat like the ox, and the serpent shall eat earth like bread. They shall not hurt nor destroy on my holy mountain, saith the Lord...'" [Is. 65:17-25] (Dialogue with Trypho, *Ibid.*).

"Better *One Day* in your courts than *a thousand* elsewhere" (Ps. 84:11).

"On that Day you will realize that I am in the Father and *you are in Me* and I in you" (Jn. 14:20).

The Day's Beginning (The Second and Great Tribulation)

"The Day of the Lord is coming; a day of darkness and of gloom like dawn spreading over the mountains, a people numerous and mighty! ... Their like has not been from of old, nor will it be after them... before them fire devours... Like the garden of Eden is the land before them" (Jl. 2:1-3).

"The work of each will come to light, for the *Day* will disclose it. It will be revealed with fire, and the fire itself will test the quality of each one's work (1 Cor. 3:13).

"Satan will be released from his prison. He will go out to deceive the nations at the four corners of the earth, Gog and Magog, to gather them for battle" (Rv. 20:7-8), etc.

The Day's Peak and Eternity (Second Triumph)

"...I shall not drink again the fruit of the vine until *the Day* when I drink it new in the kingdom of God" (Mk. 14:25).

"During the *day* its gates shall never be shut, and there will be no night... for the Lord God shall give them light, and they shall reign forever and ever" (Rv. 21:25; 22:5).

From these doctrines and scriptural passages, one can safely conclude that the thousand years which are as *a Day*, will last for a definite period, which we cannot calculate according to our standards of time. We can, on the other hand, deduce that the *Day's* commencement will be occasioned by a tribulation and last throughout the saints' reign in God's temporal kingdom. In this kingdom, moreover, the just will be granted the consolation of a "Sabbath rest".

What follows this temporal kingdom is the definitively established kingdom, which will have no end: the New Jerusalem come down from heaven. We shall treat this eternal kingdom in our next chapter. For now we may simply add that this New Jerusalem, constituent of an eternal and definitive dwelling of God with men, is evidenced in Scripture and reiterated in recent statements of our Holy Father when equating this kingdom to "the fullness of time" (thereby placing it beyond time): *"The fullness of time* is in fact eternity" (*Tertio Millennio Adveniente, Ibid.*, 9); "Christians are called to prepare for the Great Jubilee of the beginning of the Third Millennium by renewing their hope in the *definitive* coming of the *Kingdom of God...*" (*Ibid.*, 46). And inasmuch as the laws that govern time will be altered in the temporal kingdom, it may also be considered as pertinent to this fullness of time, to which our current estimation of time cannot be ascribed.

1.21. The Millennium in the Gospel of Matthew

"...tell us, when will this happen, and what sign will there be of your coming, and of the end of the age?" (Mt. 24:3).

Here we find ourselves faced with three questions: I) "when will *the destruction of the temple* occur?"; II) "what sign will there be of *his coming?*" III) "what sign will there be of *the end of the age?*" They all find their individual responses in the following verses presented in the proper chronological sequence:

III) "What sign will there be of *the end of the age?*" Mt. 24:6-14: "You will hear of wars and reports of wars; see that you are not alarmed, for these things must happen, but it will not yet be the end. Nation will rise against nation, and kingdom against kingdom; there will be famines and earthquakes from place to place. All these things are the beginning of the labor pains. Then they will hand you over to persecution, and they will kill you. You will be hated by all nations because of My name. And then many will be led into sin; they will betray and hate one another. Many false prophets will arise and deceive many, and because of the increase of evildoing, the love of many will grow cold. But the one who perseveres to the end will be saved. **And this gospel of the kingdom will be preached throughout the world as a witness to all nations,** *and then* the end will come."

Here Jesus indicates the signs that are to precede the temporal kingdom. In these first verses of Matthew's 24th chapter, Jesus implicitly treats the millennium in a manner congruent with that of the Fathers. When speaking of the kingdom, the Fathers unanimously attribute to it the characteristic of gospel universality based upon such scriptural verses: "See, the Lord proclaims to the *ends of the earth*: Say to daughter Zion, 'Your savior comes!'" (Is. 62:11); "...they shall proclaim my glory *among the nations*'"(cf. Is. 66:19), and so forth.

This gospel of which Matthew speaks, we know, has not yet been so effectively preached *throughout the world* (Mt. 24:14) and to *all nations* (Mk. 13:10) that among them the *glory* of God is proclaimed. Such a phenomenon can only be achieved by Christ Jesus when he comes in his glorified Spirit to establish his reign upon the earth, the reign of his divine will, thereby fulfilling the 2000 year-old *Pater Noster*: "Thy will be done *on earth* as it is in heaven."

I) "When will *the destruction of the temple* occur?" Mt. 24:15-21: "**When you see the desolating abomination spoken of through Daniel the prophet standing in the holy place** (let the reader understand), then those in Judea must flee to the mountains, a person on the housetop must not go down to get things out of his house, a person in the field must not return to get his cloak. Woe to the pregnant women and nursing mothers in those days. Pray that your flight not be in winter or on the Sabbath, for at that time there will be great tribulation, such as has not been since the beginning of the world until now, nor

ever will be."

The "desolating abomination" of which Jesus speaks refers to Daniel's three passages. While according to Daniel, this abomination results in a reign limited to a period of approximately 1,260 days, he refers to Satan whom the Fathers say will have two reprisals. The first, as we have seen, will precede the millennium and occur via the person of the Antichrist, with a reign of 1,260 days. The second will be the last decisive battle of Satan with Almighty God, the "Great Tribulation". This is further evidenced by God's angel who reveals to John the mystery of the great harlot whom he had already beheld in a vision: "The beast... existed once... and yet it will come again" (Rv. 17:8).

Daniel attests to Satan's first reprisal in stating that at the first rebellion (Antichrist), there will be various signs accompanying his temporary reign, all of which will appear to indicate that the end is still far off: "The nation's wise shall instruct the many; though *for a time* they will be victims of the sword, of flames, exile, and plunder... of the wise men, some shall fall, so that the rest may be tested, refined, and purified, until the end time *which is still appointed to come"* (Dn. 11:33-35).

As for the "holy place" wherein the first abomination abides, this has been traditionally designated by many scholars as the center of Christianity — in modern terms, the Church in Rome. Most scriptural scholars agree that the "holy city" with seven hills upon which the great harlot sits is none other than Rome itself. It is understood that here, in the city of the Popes, Antichrist will choose to establish his universal sovereignty: "The woman whom you saw represents the great city that has sovereignty over the kings of the earth" (Rv. 17:18).

The "harlot", for her part, is seen to be riding on both "the beast" (Rv. 17:3) and "the seven hills" (Rv. 17:9), thereby signifying the close affinity between Antichrist (whom the

Fathers consider "the beast") and his empire. It is this papal city— the holy place, God's "holy city" and "dwelling" — that Antichrist desecrates for the duration of approximately 1,260 days: "...exclude the outer court of the temple; do not measure it, for it has been given over to the Gentiles, who will trample *the holy city* for forty-two months" (Rv. 11:2); "The beast was given a mouth uttering proud boasts and blasphemies, and it was given authority to act for forty-two months. It opened its mouth to utter blasphemies against God, blaspheming his name and *his dwelling* and those who dwell in heaven" (Rv. 13:5-6). The forty-two months of which John speaks are understood as being identical with the following texts: Dn. 7:25; Rv. 12:14: "a year, two years, and a half-year"; Rv. 11:3, 12:6: "twelve hundred and sixty days".

It is also clear from Sacred Scripture that during this first period of desecration, there will be attempts to completely abolish the perpetual sacrifice of the Mass: "...he shall abolish sacrifice and oblation" (Dn. 9:27); "...sin replaced the daily sacrifice" (Dn. 8:12). Having deceived the inhabitants of the earth with the signs it was allowed to perform, Antichrist — the "beast" in the Books of Revelation and Daniel according to the Fathers — will erect a pagan image for all to worship. This image will be held on high for all to see and worship as it represents the desolating abomination's ephemeral victory over God and his holy place. After the period of approximately 1,260 days, Jesus will send forth his Spirit to transform and sanctify the earth and thus inaugurate the period of peace prophesied from of old, the millennium. At the final coming of Satan, the attempts to completely abolish the Mass will be even more vehement.

Matthew rejoins Mark with the same Greek phrase (Mt. 24:15; Mk. 13:14):

$$\text{τὸ βδέλυγμα τῆς ἐρημώσεως}$$

and places the second abomination at the end of the

millennium, at the moment of the second and "Great Tribulation": "For at that time there will be great tribulation, such as has not been since the beginning of the world until now, *nor ever will be*" (Mt. 24:21); "For those times will have tribulation such as has not been since the beginning of God's creation until now, *nor ever will be*" (Mk. 13:19). Matthew and Mark intimate that the contriver will occupy the temple, desecrating and profaning it. This temple not only refers to the one which was destroyed by fire in 70 A.D., but to another temple transcending its devastation, a fact attested to on grounds of their reference to the eschatological end time.

The prophet Ezekiel, moreover, indicates the rebuilding of Jerusalem during the millennium and, like Lactantius, testifies to its invasion by the evil one who, toward its termination, is permitted to "surround" and "besiege" the holy place. In Ezekiel chapters 38 and 39, Ezekiel describes Gog's besieging of this beloved city with the following characteristics: this invasion occurs only "after *many days...in the last years*" and is against a community "that survived the *sword...*that has been *assembled...* who dwell in *security...* a *peaceful people...* whose *ruins were repeopled* and a people *gathered from the* nations who dwell *at the navel of the earth*" (Ez. 38:8,11-12). Earlier in this chapter, we saw that these very characteristics are identical to those of the community of the first remnant, who survived the first tribulation. Gog, therefore, having invaded this beloved city, will then incite the final battle against the Most High (the second tribulation), who will allow fire to come down from heaven to consume Gog and his minions, and Satan will be cast into the pool of fire and brimstone forever (Rv. 20:9-11, 15). God's eternal victory shall then be celebrated in the established New heavens and New earth (Ez. 40).

Regarding the holy place itself, it is not to be understood so much as the physical edifice upon Mount Zion in the heart of the city, as much as the inhabitants of the city, "...the camp of the holy ones and the beloved city" (Rv. 20:9).

God will dwell in the hearts of the elect who will together form the "city of God" whose sole law will be that of love.

Like Matthew, Mark speaks of the inhabitants of Judea fleeing to the mountains, thus indicating what the early Fathers regard as the contriver's second and final rebellion: "When you see *the desolating abomination* standing where he should not (let the reader understand), then those in Judea must flee to the mountains..." (Mk. 13:14). Mark's use of a masculine participle "standing" (*hestekota*) in the neuter noun may suggest that an evil individual such as Gog may be a part of Satan's final "desolation of abomination", which can also be considered the "spirit of Antichrist". Antichrist as a person is also correctly referred to as (or causing) the desolation of abomination, as was Antiochus IV Epiphanes, the Syrian king who profaned the temple in 167 B.C.

We know from Scripture and Tradition that the end of history will occur with the invasion of the temporary kingdom, known as the "the camp of the holy ones and the beloved city" (Rv. 20:9). Gog and his followers from Magog shall be gathered together by Satan to invade this beloved city for the final and cosmic battle. Ezekiel designates Gog as the ruler of the land of Magog and chief prince of Mosoch and Tubal (Ez. 38:1-2). They shall muster up their strength and wage war against the Church, whose temple is situated on Mount Zion in Jerusalem. However, before this Great Tribulation takes place, during the millennium a host of nations will stream toward the temple:

> To you we owe our hymn of praise, O God on Zion... happy the chosen ones you bring to dwell in your courts... of your holy temple... You *visit* the earth and water it, make it abundantly fertile... (Ps. 65:2.5.10).

We read in Revelation that these nations which come to the temple to offer God homage and worship are none other than those souls who have survived the first tribulation. Indeed, once their city, their temple, has been invaded by the desolating abomination, it will signal God's final intervention in human history, the end of the temple (that is, the physical edifice, which will then give rise to the spiritual temple), and the inauguration of the New heavens and New earth: "Then I saw a new heaven and a new earth... I also saw the holy city, a new Jerusalem, coming down out of heaven from God...*I saw no temple in the city, for its temple is the Lord God almighty and the Lamb*" (Rv. 21:1-2, 22).

II) "What sign will there be of *his coming?*" Mt. 24:29-31: "Immediately after the tribulation of those days, the sun will be darkened, and the moon will not give its light, and the stars will fall from the sky, and the powers of the heavens will be shaken. **And then the sign of the Son of Man will appear in heaven,** and all the tribes of the earth will mourn, and they will see the Son of Man coming upon the clouds of heaven with power and great glory. And he will send out his angels with a trumpet blast, and they will gather his elect from the four winds, from one end of the heavens to the other."

As we have seen in the second instance, Christ's coming in the flesh for the Final Judgment will be ushered in by a trumpet blast and will follow the last reprisal of Satan who has newly "invaded the breadth of the earth and surrounded the camp of the holy ones and the beloved city" (Rv. 20:9).

1.22. Sequence of Events

God's plan for refreshment and then eternal renewal is rooted in Sacred Scripture and in the Apostolic Tradition, and it is perhaps best reflected in the following quotation of the Church Father, Saint Irenaeus of Lyons:

> **After the times of the kingdom,** he says, "I saw
> a great white throne, and Him who sat on it,
> from whose face the earth fled away, and the

heavens; and there was no more place for them" [Rv. 20:11]. Moreover, he says, "The book of life was opened and **the dead were judged...**" And **after this,** he says, **"I saw a new heaven and a new earth,** for the first heavens and earth had passed away and the sea was no more. And I saw the holy city, new Jerusalem coming down from heaven... And I heard a great voice from the throne, saying behold, the great tabernacle of God with men, and he will dwell with them" [Rv. 21:1-4]...

He [man] shall be actually disciplined beforehand for incorruption, **and shall go forwards** and flourish **in the times of the kingdom,** in order that he may be capable of receiving the glory of the Father. **Then,** when **all things are made new,** he shall truly dwell in the city of God. For it is said, "He that sitteth on the throne said, Behold, I make all things new" [Rv. 21:5] (Adversus Haereses, *Ibid.*, passim Bk. 5, Ch. 35).

N.B. Irenaeus clearly distinguishes the four events that are to follow: first *man shall be disciplined* (**the first tribulation**); then will come *the times of the kingdom* (**the millennium**); followed by the judgment of *all the dead* (**the aftermath of the second tribulation**); and finally *the New Jerusalem* (**the New heavens and New earth**).

Based on the Apostolic Tradition as developed through the combined scholarship of the early Church Fathers and Doctors, the eschatological events will unfold as follows:

- first tribulation (Antichrist)

- first instance of General Judgment and abolishment of all the earth's evildoers

- temporal kingdom or era of peace (transformed heavens and earth)

- Great Tribulation (Gog, Prince of Magog)

- resurrection of all bodies

- second instance of General Judgment

- New heavens and New earth

In concluding our section dedicated to the millennium, as evidenced in Sacred Scripture and the doctrines of the Church Fathers and Doctors, we cannot overlook their dogmatic contribution that has enriched the Church for centuries. Since their writings rejoin the main current of Apostolic Tradition, they form a developed doctrine that organically unites itself to the deposit of faith. Based upon the tenor of these ancients' writings – rooted in Scripture and wholly governed by the Tradition received from the Apostles – the Magisterium has confirmed their theological contribution and has allowed the faithful to draw knowledge from them. The homogeneity of their writings is evidenced in their development of doctrine regarding the nature of God's temporal kingdom. And as we have seen, this progress in doctrine has been guided by the Holy Spirit. It is the Spirit's guidance that aids in the development of Tradition through the earliest writers to the most recent. This collective succession of common doctrines, known in theology as the *analogy of faith,* is the relationship of the various truths combined through the centuries that form one center of revelation, the Catholic Tradition.

CHAPTER 6

CHARACTERISTICS OF THE NEW JERUSALEM

After the second instance of the General Judgment, the earth will be eternally renewed. This marks the end of human history and the descent of the New Jerusalem in all its glory from heaven, God's permanent abode with his creatures in Paradise repossessed.

1.1. Christ's Eternal Dwelling *With* Men

"Then He shall indeed rest on the seventh day... You see what He means... that Sabbath which I have made, in which, *after* giving rest to all things, I will make the beginning of the eighth day, that is, the beginning of another world" (Letter of Barnabas, *Ibid.*).

"The followers of Christ would dwell in Jerusalem for a thousand years, and that *afterwards* the universal and, in short, everlasting resurrection and judgment would take place" (Dialogue with Trypho, *Ibid.*).

"The King of Israel is in your midst, you have no further misfortune to fear..." (Zep. 3:15).

"I heard a loud voice from the throne saying, 'Behold, God's dwelling is with the human race. He will dwell with them and they will be his people and God himself will always be with them'... They will look upon his face... and they shall reign forever and ever" (Rv. 21:3; 22:4-5).

Unlike Christ's reign *over* the earth during the millennium, the New Jerusalem will affirm Christ as its Lord and king who will reign *with* his saints, as is particularly evidenced in the following scriptural texts: "Then he [Jacob] had a dream: a stairway rested on the ground, with its top reaching to the heavens; and God's messengers were going up and down on it. And there was the Lord standing beside him and saying: 'I, the Lord, am God... Know that I am with you; I will protect you wherever you go" (Gn. 28:12-15); "Jesus answered and said to him... 'Amen, amen, I say to you, you will see the sky opened and the angels of God ascending and descending on the Son of Man'" (Jn. 1:50, 51); "The throne of God and of the Lamb will be in it [the New Jerusalem], and his servants will worship him" (Rv. 22:3).

Christ's eternal reign among all the just in the New heavens and New earth will not resemble those carnal banquets or immoderate pleasures so often associated with the erroneous doctrine of millenarianism, "For the kingdom of God is not a matter of food and drink, but of righteousness, peace and joy in the Holy Spirit" (Rom. 14:17). The New Jerusalem, therefore, unlike the preceding millennium, entertains no inventions of further struggles or divisions. There will cease all alternations of light and darkness (all darkness will be banished); all tensions between grace and sin (all will live in perfect accord with God's Divine Will); the division of the heavens and earth (there will be New heavens and New earth as in the original paradisal state of perfect oneness with God). The New heavens and New earth, marked by the sublime fusion of the spiritual and the material orders, will forever rejoice with the sons of God, who partake in an unveiled and eternal communion with the angels and their Creator.

1.2. Eternal Rest; the Eighth Day

"You see what He means... that Sabbath which I have made, in which, after giving rest to all things, I will make *the beginning of the eighth day*, that is, the beginning of another world" (Letter of Barnabas, *Ibid.*).

"...The followers of Christ would dwell in Jerusalem for a thousand years, and that *afterwards* the universal and, in short, everlasting resurrection and judgment would take place. To this our Lord himself testified when He said: 'They shall neither marry, nor be given in marriage, but shall be equal to the angels, being sons of God, (that is) of the resurrection'" (Dialogue with Trypho, *Ibid.*).

"*After* its thousand years are over, within which period is completed the resurrection of the saints... there will ensue the destruction of the world and the conflagration of all things at the judgment: we shall *then* be changed in a moment into the substance of angels, even by the investiture of an incorruptible nature, and so be removed to that kingdom in heaven [the New Jerusalem]" (Adversus Marcion, *Ibid.*).

"But *when the thousand years shall be completed*, the world shall be renewed by God, and the heavens shall be folded together, and the earth shall be changed, and God shall transform men into the similitude of angels, and they shall be white as snow; and they shall always be employed in the sight of the Almighty, and shall make offerings to their Lord, and serve Him forever" (The Divine Institutes, *Ibid.*).

St. Methodius, unlike the Fathers' analogy of the seven days of creation, adopts the text of Leviticus, which treats the Feast of Tabernacles. He allegorically interprets this feast to be the "Eighth Day" of creation. Therefore, he goes so far as to call this eighth day that has no end "the true Sabbath". This "true Sabbath" is not, however, to be equated with the Fathers' doctrines on the "Sabbath Rest". Rather, Methodius intended to express the existence of that kingdom which knows no end that which the Fathers speak of as possessing those abiding characteristics which differ from the millennium. In short, Methodius presents us with that eternal "Day of the Lord" which has no end, the New Jerusalem. The following are the traits which he ascribes to the "true Sabbath":

> The New creation... when this world shall have come to an end... and the sun no longer rises to rule the day, nor the moon the night... when the world comes to an end in fire... when the truth will be fulfilled at the Second Coming of Christ... when all our tabernacles will be established, when our bodies rise again... Then we shall celebrate to the Lord... receiving now eternal tabernacles, never more to die or to be dissolved into the earth of the grave... Thus with sin dead and destroyed... I will celebrate the Feast in His honor... on the first day, the day, that is, on which I am judged... In the New creation where pain will be unknown... into the Promise (sic) Land... the Holy Land... (The Symposium, *Ibid.*, pp. 131-140).

As can be gleaned from his writings, St. Methodius concurs with the early Fathers in appropriating to the New Jerusalem such traits as fire cleansing and renewing the earth, the resurrection of all the dead, the cessation of the sun and the moon, the destruction of sin and death once and for all, etc. Thus Methodius' terms of "a New creation", "the Seventh Month", "the Promise (sic) Land", etc. all refer to the eternal rest of God with men.

1.3. Resurrection of All the Dead

"But your dead shall live, their corpses shall rise; awake and sing, you who lie in the dust" (Is. 26:19).

"Then he said to me: 'Prophesy over these bones, and say to them: Dry bones, hear the word of the Lord! Thus says the Lord God to these bones: See! I will bring spirit into you, that you may come to life. I will put sinews upon you, make flesh grow over you, cover you with skin, and put spirit in you so that you come to life and know that I am the Lord... when I open your graves and have you rise from them... and I will settle you upon your land'" (Ez. 37:4-14).

"I saw the dead, the great and the lowly, standing before the throne, and scrolls were opened. Then another scroll was opened, the book of life. The dead were judged according to their deeds, by what was written in the scrolls... All the dead were judged according to their deeds" (Rv. 20:12-13).

1.4. The Garden of Eden Reinhabited, but Even More Beautiful Than Before

By the divine purifying fires and an immense profusion of grace, whatever is imperfect will be purged and emerge completely renewed, more beautiful than ever, without stain or wrinkle. God will once again be pleased to display his reflection in this Paradise, once lost but never abolished. When God expelled man from the Garden of Eden, "...he settled him east of the garden... and he stationed a Cherubim and the fiery revolving sword, to guard the way to the tree of life" (Gn. 3:24). Yet, we rediscover this tree in the New Jerusalem together with the final remnant of God's chosen ones. What had once been removed from man is now restituted, but with even more beauty than before.

a. The Tree of Life

"But these things seduce the wary, who fail to realize that the tree of life which once grew in Paradise has now been made to bloom again [in the New heavens and New earth]... He (Christ) is the first principle, the 'tree of life'" (The Symposium, *Ibid.*).

"Then the Lord God planted a garden in Eden... with the tree of life in the middle..." (Gn. 2:8-9).

"To the victor I will give the right to eat from the tree of life that is in the garden of God" (Rv. 2:7).

"On either side of the river grew the tree of life... Blessed are they who have washed their robes so as to have the right to the tree of life..." (Rv. 22:2, 14).

b. Greater Beauty Than in the Beginning

"Father, in restoring human nature you have given us a greater dignity than we had in the beginning" (*The Liturgy of the Hours, Ibid.*, Vol. II, p. 791).

"Everything returns to its origin" (*Tertio Millennio Adveniente, Ibid.*, 6).

"I will be... more generous to you than in the beginning; thus you shall know that I am the Lord" (Ez. 36:11).

"Greater will be the future glory of this house than the former..." (Hg. 2:9).

1.5.   No More Sacraments

"Until there is realized new heavens and new earth...the pilgrim Church, in her Sacraments and institutions, which belong to this present age, carry the mark of this world *which will pass*..." (*CCC, Ibid.*).

"...I am with you always, *until* the end of the age" (Mt.

28:19-20).

"For as often as you eat this bread and drink the cup, you proclaim the death of the Lord *until* he comes" (1 Cor. 11:26).

1.6.   No More Death

"And again another prophet says: '...And there was a river flowing on the right hand, and beautiful trees grew of it, and whoever shall eat of them *shall live forever'*... This means: Whoever hears these things spoken and believes *shall live forever"* (Letter of Barnabas, *Ibid.*).

"'They shall neither marry, nor be given in marriage, but *shall be equal to the angels,* being sons of God, (that is) of the resurrection'" (Dialogue with Trypho, *Ibid.*).

"We shall then be changed in a moment into the substance of angels, even by the investiture of an *incorruptible nature*, and so be removed to that kingdom in heaven [the New Jerusalem]" (Adversus Marcion, *Ibid.*).

"God shall transform men into the similitude of angels, and they shall be white as snow; and they shall *always* be employed in the sight of the Almighty, and shall make offerings to their Lord, and serve Him *forever"* (The Divine Institutes, *Ibid.*).

"The Lord shall come in his majesty, and all his angels with him (cf. Mt. 25:31), and, *death having been destroyed*, all things shall be subject to him (cf. 1 Cor. 15:26-27)" (*The Christian Faith in the Documents of the Catholic Church, Ibid.*, 2312).

"...and there shall be no more death..." (Rv. 21:4).

1.7. Perpetual Light

"For a sun...is the Lord God" (Ps. 84:12).

"By day the sun cannot harm you, nor the moon by night. The Lord will guard you..." (Ps. 121:6-7).

"No longer shall the sun be your light by day, nor the brightness of the moon shine upon you at night; the Lord will be your light forever... No longer shall your sun go down, or your moon withdraw, for the Lord will be your light forever" (Is. 60:19-20).

"The city had no need of sun or moon to shine on it, for the glory of God gave it light, and its lamp was the Lamb" (Rv. 21:23-24).

"Night will be no more, nor will they need light from lamp or sun, for the Lord God shall give them light, and they shall reign forever and ever" (Rv. 22:5).

St. Thomas Aquinas speaks of the completion of the number of the elect who will resurrect (the final remnant), and the beginning of what he occasionally refers to as "the cessation of the heavenly bodies". The two events coincide, as both are dependent upon the completion of the number of the elect:

> The heavens will be broken in the sense that their movement will cease... *At the resurrection of the saints the movements of the heavenly bodies will cease.* Again, he writes: *"After the judgment the sun will receive the reward of its labor, thenceforward neither sun nor moon shall set."* I answer that following the teaching of the holy men we hold that at some time the celestial movement will cease... We hold then that the movement of the heavens is for the completion of the number of the elect... Therefore it is a

definite number of souls that is the end of the heavenly movement: and when this is reached the movement will cease (*Quaestiones Disputatae, Ibid.*).

When the heavens cease to be in motion, although *the sun will always remain to the one side of the earth,* there will be utter darkness and gloom on the other side, because God will give brightness to the elements... And no inconsistency will follow if *the part which was inhabited by the saints receive a greater* light... the heavens will cease to be in motion solely on account of the will of their mover (*Ibid.*).

N.B. This "resurrection of the saints" refers not to the first but the second resurrection. Tertullian clarifies the issue when stating that there will be a first resurrection "for a thousand years in the divinely built city of Jerusalem...," followed by a second resurrection of all the dead at the end of the thousand years: "After its thousand years are over... there will ensue the destruction of the world and the conflagration of all things at the judgment. We shall then be changed in a moment into the substance of angels, even by the investiture of an incorruptible nature, and so be removed to that kingdom in heaven [the New Jerusalem]" (Adversus Marcion, *Ibid.*).

Despite this cessation of heavenly bodies, in no way is the world's eternal existence affected. In his *Quaestiones Disputatae,* St. Thomas affirms the eternity of the created world. He states that, "The sense of the passages quoted (2 Pt. 3:10: *'The heavens shall pass away'*; Lk. 21:33: *'Heaven and earth will pass away'*) is not that the substance of the world will perish, but that its outward appearance will vanish according to the Apostle (1 Cor. 7:31)" (*Quaestiones Disputatae, Ibid.*).

1.8.   No More Sun and Moon

"He says to them: *'I will not abide your new moons and your Sabbaths.'* You see what He means: The present Sabbaths are not acceptable to Me, but that Sabbath which I have made, in which, after giving rest to all things, I will make the beginning of the eighth day, that is, the beginning of another world" (Letter of Barnabas, *Ibid.*).

"But *when the thousand years shall be completed, the world shall be renewed by God*, and the heavens shall be folded together" (The Divine Institutes, *Ibid.*).

"No longer shall the sun be your light by day, nor the brightness of the moon shine upon you at night; the Lord shall be your light forever, your God shall be your glory. No longer shall your sun go down, or your moon withdraw, for the Lord will be your light forever" (Is. 60:19-20).

"I am the light of the world... I came into the world as light..." (Jn. 8:12; 12:46).

"The city had no need of sun or moon to shine on it, for the glory of God gave it light...nor will they need light from lamp or sun, for the Lord God shall give them light and they shall reign forever and ever" (Rv. 21:23; 22:5).

1.9.   Final Remnant

As there are two tribulations, it necessarily follows that there will be two surviving remnant groups. Following are passages which refer to the *final* remnant...

"...the Lord's renown..." (Is. 55:13).

"But on Mount Zion there shall be a portion saved...And

saviors shall ascend Mount Zion..." (Ob. 1:17, 21).

"Behold, God's dwelling is with the human race. He will dwell with them and they will be his people and God himself will always be with them..." (Rv. 21:3).

1.10.   No More Sin

"See that we shall then indeed sanctify it when we enjoy true repose... because we have been made just ourselves and shall have received the promise, *when there is no more sin,* but all things have been made new by the Lord" (Letter of Barnabas, *Ibid.*).

"God is preparing a New dwelling place and a New earth, where justice will reign (cf. 2 Cor. 5:1; 2 Pt. 3:13)... Then, with death defeated... what had been sown in weakness and corruption will be clothed with incorruptibility (cf. 1 Cor. 15:42.53)... and this whole creation made by God for our sake will be freed from the bondage of vanity (cf. Rom. 8:9-21)...cleansed of all sin, illuminated and transfigured, when Christ will hand over to the Father an eternal and universal Kingdom" (*The Christian Faith in the Documents of the Catholic Church, Ibid.,* p. 949).

"I will make my holy name known among my people Israel; I will no longer allow my holy name to be profaned" (Ez. 39:7).

"The treasure and wealth of the nations will be brought there, but nothing unclean will enter it, nor anyone who does abominable things or tells lies... Nothing accursed will be found there anymore" (Rv. 21:26-27; 22:3).

1.11.   No Longer Is Instruction *by Men* Necessary; No More Preaching of the Gospel to All the Nations

"All your sons shall be taught by the Lord..." (Is. 54:13).

"I will place my law within them, and write it upon their hearts... No longer will they need to teach their friends and kinsmen how to know the Lord. All, from the least to the greatest, shall know me, says the Lord..." (Jer. 31:33-34).

"It is written in the prophets: 'They shall all be taught by God'" (Jn. 6:45).

"And they shall not teach their fellow citizens or brothers, saying, 'Know the Lord,' for all shall know me, from the least to the greatest" (cf. Heb. 8:11).

1.12.   Full Acquisition of the "Divine Nature"

"A man among us named John, one of Christ's Apostles, received and foretold that the followers of Christ would dwell in Jerusalem for a thousand years, and that afterwards the universal and, in short, everlasting resurrection and judgment would take place. To this our Lord himself testified when He said: 'They shall neither marry, nor be given in marriage, but *shall be equal to the angels,* being sons of God, (that is) of the resurrection'" (Dialogue with Trypho, *Ibid.*).

"After its thousand years are over, within which period is completed the resurrection of the saints... there will ensue the destruction of the world and the conflagration of all things at the judgment: we shall then be changed in a moment into the substance of angels, even *by the investiture of an incorruptible nature*, and so be removed to that kingdom in Heaven [the New Jerusalem]" (Adversus Marcion, *Ibid.*).

"But when the thousand years shall be completed, the world shall be renewed by God, and the heavens shall be folded together, and the earth shall be changed, and God shall transform men into the similitude of angels, and they shall be white as snow; and they shall always be employed in the sight of the Almighty, and shall make offerings to their Lord, and serve Him forever" (The Divine Institutes, *Ibid.*).

"Just as we have borne the image of the earthly one, we shall also bear the image of the heavenly one" (1 Cor. 15:49).

"Beloved, we are God's children now; what we shall be has not yet been revealed. We know that when it is revealed we shall be like him, for we shall see him as he is" (1 Jn. 3:2). "We shall see him as he is" is an allusion to Rv. 22:4: "They will look upon his face..."

"The divine power of Christ has freely bestowed on us everything necessary for a life of genuine piety, through knowledge of him who called us by his own glory and power. By virtue of them he has bestowed on us the great and precious things he promised, so that through these, you who have fled a world corrupted by lust *might become* sharers in the divine nature" (2 Pt. 1:3-4).

"When we have come to know the true God, both our bodies and souls will be immortal and incorruptible. Friends of God and coheirs with Christ, we shall be subject to no evil desires or inclinations, or to have any affliction of the body or soul, for we shall have become divine" (On the Refutation of all Heresies, Saint Hippolytus, in *Liturgy of the Hours, Ibid.*, p. 460).

1.13.   Cessation of Separation of Earth and Sky; Spiritual and Material Orders Reunited

"The earth and the sky fled from his presence and there was no place for them" (Rv. 20:11).

"Then I saw a new heaven and a new earth. The former heaven and the former earth *had passed away, and the sea was no more*... He took me in spirit to a great, high mountain and showed me the holy *city Jerusalem coming down out of heaven* from God... I saw no temple in the city, for its temple is the Lord God almighty and the Lamb... the river of life-giving water sparkling like crystal, flowing *from the throne of God and of the Lamb* down the middle of its street...Nothing accursed will be found there anymore. The throne of God and of the Lamb *will be in it*, and his servants shall worship him. Night will be no more, nor will they need light from lamp or the sun..." (Rv. 21:1, 10-11, 22; 22:1-3).

Here we are presented with the end of the division created by original sin. The unity that once existed in Eden, intended to last for eternity, was ruptured by man's fall into sin. It was God's plan to bring about restoration, which was only possible through the intervention of One who was above the fallen human race wounded by sin. This God-Man would be Jesus Christ.

Through his Passion, Death and Resurrection, Jesus instituted the Sacraments which would, in turn, *begin* to restore this unity to man. The Sacraments serve to reconcile the material order (the Garden of Eden, which was not changed but removed from man) with the spiritual (Heaven), in order to eventually restore the unity which creation had many centuries longed for in anxious expectation of the sons of God. With his coming in the flesh in glory, however, Christ will definitively restore all things to their original state of union with the Father, thereby ending once and for all the division caused by original sin.

This process of redemption and universal unification of all creation can be gleaned from the writings of many outstanding scholars. In these approaching days of the third millennium, the Great Jubilee, the Holy Spirit has apparently sent several inspired and holy theologians to positively shape our understanding of the things to come. This scholarship, or branch of theology known as *eschatology,* deals especially with the Last Things.

To summarize this wholesome development of such renowned scholars would take some doing. But if we avail ourselves of the general thrust of these writings, we may begin by saying that in the beginning of time, when God created Light, he separated it from darkness. However, in order that a creative and material order should exist, he united the two. It wasn't until after Adam's sin that God further distanced light from darkness, water from dry land, heavens from earth, and allowed the separation of grace from sin. This process of division was later made manifest in the formation of the Church in her opposition to the world.

However, by Jesus' abandonment to the Father's Will and through his return in glory, he removes the distance between the material and spiritual orders; by his assuming the effects of sin for our redemption and the world's renewal, he allowed "light to shine in the darkness" (cf. Jn. 1:5), showers of grace to once again permeate the cursed, arid land into which Adam and his sons were exiled; which will culminate in the New heavens and New earth to rejoice forever "with the throne of God and the Lamb in their midst" (cf. Rv. 22:3). The New heavens and New earth will, therefore, assume a form similar to that possessed in the paradisal state in which all fecundity came into the world through the primacy of spirit and love. The relationship of nature and grace will fluctuate wherein grace willingly submits to the laws of nature; and nature finds its fulfillment in being drawn above itself and thus restored to the original idea of its creation.

1.14. Sequence of Events

- First tribulation and first instance of the General Judgment of all the living (Christ descends from heaven in his glorified Spirit, a sword of judgment issues from his mouth, and it occurs suddenly, in an hour/Day) — the first fruits of the remnant possess the temporal kingdom.

- Great Tribulation and second instance of the General Judgment of the dead (Christ comes in the flesh in glory, and is seen with his Father pronouncing sentences of righteousness and condemnation from their throne, accompanied by fire) — the final remnant possesses the New Jerusalem forever and ever.

CHAPTER 7

CONCLUSION

As evidenced in Sacred Scriptures, the writings of Church Fathers, Doctors and ecclesiastical writers, and in statements issued from her ordinary Magisterium, references to the millennium or temporal kingdom of God have one common thread: the veritable reality of a period of peace that precedes the great and universal day of Final Judgment of all the dead.

These writings are unwavering in their doctrinal fidelity to traditional Church teachings, which thus attests to their truthfulness. As our Holy Father has so often quoted, this millennium will be marked by "a new springtime in Christianity," will be "intensely Eucharistic," at its dawn will "make Christ the heart of the world," and will have as its "*goal* and *fulfillment...* the life of each Christian and the whole Church in the Triune God" (passim *Tertio Millennio Adveniente, Ibid.*).

While concurring in the condemnation of *millenarianism*, the heresy ever ancient and ever new, these writings unanimously testify to the characteristics unique to that temporal kingdom wherein God will rest in the hearts of all the earth's inhabitants. They, in turn, like living hosts, will carry him in their hearts and follow the Lamb wherever he goes. Utilizing the proper tools for biblical exegesis, and the various modes of expression applied thereto, the doctrines of the early

165

Fathers are recognized for their outstanding orthodoxy. Far from being enigmatic in nature, they are found to be impeccably unanimous and consistent with the Tradition they received and faithfully transmitted to us from the Apostles. The term "enigmatic" is better applied to those writers who have not fully grasped the theological significance of the term *millenarianism,* which constitutes a specific heresy with peculiar traits totally unlike the unmodified doctrines of the Fathers.

In these latter days on the threshold of the third millennium, disputes inevitably arise in spite of the Church's authoritative voice. Although she possesses the power to either close the matter or allow for further doctrinal development in its clarification, Holy Mother Church has nonetheless opted for the latter. She has assumed a cautious position with regard to the concept of a millennium, due primarily to the resurgent tendencies of the past that have most commonly led to a slippery slope quest for *millenarianism.* However, understood in a *spiritual sense,* the question of a millennium or temporal kingdom as promoted through the "spiritual" writings of the Church Fathers remains open to a definitive pronouncement by the Magisterium. In the words of Cardinal Joseph Ratzinger: *"Giacché la Santa Sede non si é ancora pronunciata in modo definitivo"* ["the Holy See has not yet made any definitive pronouncement in this regard"].

This distinction in terms cannot be overstated; the omission of the simple clarification of the different doctrines on the *temporal kingdom* and *millenarianism* has precipitated into a dialectic war in which Catholic subjects are placed in opposing camps, each insufficiently armed for battle. Lack of scholarship has taken the high ground, seeming to be the victor in the onslaught of falsified doctrines — the victor that is, if not for the Holy Spirit's assistance in guiding the Church to the truth in all things.

Although the fullness of the truth currently suffers

through the ongoing and undergoing martyrdom of the pen, the truth will eventually manifest itself as perhaps in the days of Noah, even if it is only after the flood waters have arrived. So despite those authors who, under the guidance of the historian Eusebius, have thrown out the possibility of a true millennium, God, at the opportune moment, will make manifest what is hidden, and bring to light what is undisclosed. The exchangeable usage of both terms along with the ubiquitous stigma it received at the hands of eusebian ideologues have caused these authors to "miss the boat" in their assessment of the Fathers' unmodified doctrines.

The ambiguities and ambivalencies generated by their writings have led to extreme apathy in others who simply "abandoned ship", expressing no desire to discern their peculiar significance in the vein of the Apostolic Tradition; for that matter, they have deserted the quest to discover exactly what the Church had condemned in the heresy of *millenarianism.* Needless to say, the weeds sown among the faithful worked to the detriment of Tradition and doctrinal orthodoxy. Subsequently, a fear and even a paranoia regarding the doctrines of a *true* millennium has emerged, caused not by Tradition, but by a long-standing neglect to comprehend the deeper meaning of the literary contributions of ancient Christian writers whom the Catholic Church calls to bear witness to her doctrine.

The sincere but unscholarly evaluation of these writings that accrue to the Catholic Tradition are the scapegoat. And unless this goat is sacrificed, there can be neither a cleansing nor an enlightenment of consciences regarding our Lord's economy of salvation. Yet, such an enlightenment is necessary if ever his kingdom is to manifest itself in all its glory: "The approaching end of the second millennium demands of everyone an examination of consciences... so that we can celebrate the Great Jubilee... overcoming the divisions of the second millennium" (*Tertio Millennio Adveniente, Ibid.*, 34).

By means of the Tradition given to us by the Apostles and transmitted to the Apostolic Fathers, God's plan for humankind is gradually disclosed in, by and for the Church as she continues in her doctrinal development, progressing along the winding road of salvation history.

> Indeed, the Church, though scattered throughout the world, even to the ends of the earth, having *received the faith from the Apostles and their disciples*... guards [this preaching] with care, as dwelling in a single house, and similarly believes as if having but one soul and a single heart, and preaches, teaches, and hands on this faith with a unanimous voice, as if possessing only one mouth (*CCC, Ibid.*, 173).

The recent rediscovery of the Apostolic Fathers' doctrines, has effected a greater searching for the truth in all its forms. And the truth, Jesus tells us, is the expression of a love, of which no greater love is conceivable. It is reserved for mere children, whom love enables to participate in the freedom of the sons of God. Remaining open to the love of the Holy Spirit, who alone can bring about the renewal of creation, and to whom the Holy Father dedicated 1998, will enable him by way of his sevenfold gifts, to bring about greater knowledge and understanding of the Father's Will (to whom he dedicated 1999) in these end times.

"Our Father, who art in heaven; hallowed be thy name. Thy Kingdom come; thy Will be done on earth as it is in heaven." And so it shall be.

EPILOGUE

We believe you have been blessed with information that few people possess. Please share it with others for God's glory. If you found this book to be helpful or valuable, please recommend it to your friends and family. This book can be a great evangelization tool to help awaken many from their spiritual lethargy.

This book can also help people who: mistakenly believe that Christ will come in the flesh to live on the earth in the year 2000; or who mistakenly believe the world will end in the year 2000; or who mistakenly believe that good Christians will be "raptured" away prior to any chastisement.

God's true message, as this book authoritatively demonstrates, is one of Hope.

A personal Antichrist will come, and all evildoers will be judged. However, the world will continue with true peace among men due to an outpouring of the Holy Spirit. Some Christians will be "caught up in the air to meet the Lord"; but this will not happen until the end of the world, after the final coming of Satan, when our Lord will come back in his glorified flesh to reunite all bodies with their souls and pronounce the Final Judgment. For our own good, God has chosen to keep this date to himself.

Please help us reach as many people as possible with this important and timely work! God will richly bless you for it.

BIBLIOGRAPHY

Acta Apostolicae Sedis, 36, Rome, 1944.

Adversus Haereses, Irenaeus of Lyons, *The Fathers of the Church,* CIMA Publishing Co., NY, 1947.

Adversus Marcion, Tertullian, *Ante-Nicene Fathers,* Henrickson Pub., Peabody, MA, 1995.

A History of Early Christian Doctrine,Before the Council of Nicea, Jean Danielou, London, Darton, Longman & Todd, Westminster Press, Philadelphia, PA, 1964.

Ananstasii Abbatis, Sanctae Romanae Ecclesiae Presbiteri et Bibliothecarii, Opera Omnia, Anastasius of Sinai, accurante J.P. Migne, Lutetiae Parisiorum, Migne, 1852.

A New Catechism — Catholic Faith for Adults, Herder and Herder, NY, 1969.

Apologia del Cristianesimo, Tertullian, *Ante-Nicene Fathers,* Henrickson Pub., Peabody, MA, 1995.

Articolo sul Millenarianismo, *Il Grande Dizionario delle Religione,* Paul Poupard, Cittadella Editrice, Assisi, Italy, 1990.

Augustine's "Millenarianism" Reconsidered, J. Kevin Coyle, *Augustinus 38,* 1993.

Catechism of the Catholic Church, Libreria Editrice Vaticana, St. Paul Books & Media, 1994.

Catechism of the Council of Trent, Christian Press Co., NY, 1905.

Catholic Dictionary , Macmillan Co., 1941.

Catholic Dictionary of Dogmatic Theology, Bruce Publishing Co., Milwaukee, WI, 1952.

Catholic Encyclopedia, Sunday Visitor Pub., Huntington, IN, 1991.

Catholic Encyclopedia Revised, Nashville, TN, Thomas Nelson, 1987.

Chronikon, syntomon ex diaphoron chronographon te kai exegeton synlegen kai syntheom upo Georgiou Monachou tou epikale Hamartolou, Lipsiae, Parisiorum, 1863.

Codex Vaticanus Alexandrinus, Nr. 14 Bibl. Lat., Romae, 1747.

Commonitory of 434, Vincent of Lérins, *Patrology,* Johannes Quasten, Spectrum Pub., Utrecht—Brussels, 1850.

Cursus Patrologiae, Omnium SS. Patrum Ecclesiasticorum, Archiepiscopi Caesarae Cappadociae, *Commentarius in Joannis Theologi Apocalypsin,* Tomus Unicus, J.P. Migne Editorem, Paris, 1863.

De Civitate Dei [The City of God], Augustine of Hippo, Catholic University of America Press, Washington, 3rd Printing, 1977.

De Romano Pontefice, Robert Bellarmine, Neapoli, apud Josephum Giuliano, 1856.

Dei Verbum, Vatican Council II, Costello Pub. Co., Northport, NY, Rev. Ed., 1988.

De Viris Illustribus, St. Jerome, 18, Sansoni, Firenze, 1964.

Dialogue with Trypho, Justin Martyr, *The Fathers of the*

Church, Christian Heritage, 1948.

Dictionary of the Bible, Bruce Pub. Co., Milwaukee, WI, 1965.

Discussions and Arguments on Various Subjects, John Henry Newman, Basil Montagu Pickering, London, 1872.

E imminente una nuova era di vita cristiana?, Padre Martino Penasa, *Il Segno del Soprannaturale,* Udine, Italia, 1990

Enchiridion Symbolorum, Heinrich Denzinger, 423, cura di Johannes B. Umberg SJ, 1951.

Enchiridion Symbolorum, definitionum et declarationum de rebus fidei et morum, Heinrich Denzinger, 3839, cura di Peter Hünermann, Barcinone, Herder Pub., 1965 [ed. Dehoniane Bologna 1995].

Enciclopedia Cattolica, Città del Vaticano, Ente per l'Enciclopedia Cattolica e per il libro Cattolico, 1948.

Encyclopedia of the Early Church, Vol. II, Edited by Angelo DiBerardino, James Clarke & Co., Cambridge, England, 1992.

Epitome Historiarum, 471/5, Lipsiac, Teubner, 1868.

Gaudium et Spes, Vatican Council II, Costello Pub. Co., Northport, NY, Revised Ed., 1988.

Georgii Monachi Chronicon, in aedibus B.G. Teubneri, Lipsiae, Parisiorum, 1904.

Historiae 7,18 Lipsiac, Teubner, 1887.

Jerome Biblical Commentary, J.A. Fitzmeyer, Prentice-Hall, Engelwood Cliffs, NJ, 1968.

La Somma Teologica, IV Sent., Thomas Aquinas, edizione Studio Domenicano, Bologna, 1985.

La Typologie du sabbat chez saint Augustin. Son interprétation millenariste entre 389 et 400, G. Folliet, Revue études Augustiniennes II, 1956.

Letter of Barnabas, *The Fathers of the Church,* CIMA Co., NY, 1947.

Letter on the Centenary of the Rogationist Fathers, Pope John Paul II, in *L'Osservatore Romano,* Vatican City, English ed., July 9, 1997.

Lumen Gentium, Vatican Council II, Costello Pub. Co., Northport, NY, Revised Ed., 1988.

Mille ans de bonheur. Une histoire du paradis, J. Delumeau, Paris, 1995.

New Catholic Encyclopedia, McGraw-Hill Pub., NY, 1967.

On the Threshold of a New Era, Cardinal Joseph Ratzinger, Ignatius Press, San Francisco, CA, 1996.

Patrologiae Graeca, Jacques Paul Migne, Paris, 1857.

Patrology, Berthold Altaner, Herder and Herder, NY, 1961.

Quaestiones Disputatae, Vol. II *De Potentia,* Q.5, Art. 5, Editrice Marietti, Roma, Italy, 1965.

Septuaginta, 1d est Vetus Testamentum graece iuxta LXX interpretes; edidit Alfred Rahls; Duo volumina in uno; Deutsche Bibelgesellschaft, Stuttgart, Germany, 1979.

Summa Theologica, Thomas Aquinas, editio quarta, Lethielleux, Parisiis, 1939.

Tertio Millennio Adveniente, Inside the Vatican, Martin de Porres Printshop, New Hope, KY, 1994.

The Book of Destiny, H.B. Kramer, TAN Books and Publishers, Inc., Rockford, IL, 1975.

The Christian Faithful, Society of St. Paul, 6th Ed., 1995.

The Christian Faith in the Documents of the Catholic Church, J. Neuner & J. Dupuis, Harper Collins, London, 1995.

The Divine Institutes, Lactantius, *Ante-Nicene Fathers*, Henrickson Pub., Peabody, MA, 1995.

The Faith Explained, Leo John Trese, Fides Pub. Assn., Chicago, IL, 1959.

The Faith of the Early Fathers, W.A. Jurgens, Liturgical Press, Collegeville, MN, 1970.

The Fragments of Papias, Papias of Hierapolis, in *The Fathers of the Church*, CIMA Publishing Co., NY, 1947.

The Liturgy of the Hours, Catholic Book Publishing Co., NY, Vol. I-IV, 1975.

The Meaning of Tradition, Yves Congar, Hawthorn Books, NY, 1964.

The New Greek-English New Testament, Tyndale House Publishers, Wheaton, IL, 1990.

The Symposium, Methodius, Logos 9, in *Ancient Christian Writers*, The Newman Press, Westminster, MD, Ed. Quasten & Plumpe, 1958.

The Teaching of the Catholic Church: A Summary of Catholic Doctrine, Burns Oates & Washbourne, London, 1952.

Utopia the Perennial Heresy, Thomas Steven Molnar, Sheed & Ward, NY, 1967.

ABOUT THE AUTHOR

Joseph Iannuzzi is a Roman Catholic Priest in the order of the Oblates of St. Joseph. He has a Master's Degree in Theology, and is currently studying for a Doctorate in Sacred Theology at the Gregorian University in Rome, Italy.

How to Order Additional Copies of this Book:

To place an order for this book, please contact the bookstore or catalog from which it was originally purchased. If not, call toll-free:

St. Andrew's Productions
1-888-654-6279
www.saintandrew.com
or write to:
St. Andrew's Productions
6111 Steubenville Pike
McKees Rocks, PA 15136

Quantity discounts are available to individuals for evangelization purposes. Please call for rates.